Other titles from Dr. Nathaniel Stampley, Sr.

Introduction to Homiletics

Understanding Spiritual Gifts and Calling to Ministry

Biblical Commentary on Wisdom Literature

Parables of The Kingdom

Copyright © 2017 Nathaniel Stampley

Spiritscribe Publishing, LLC
P.O. Box 2241
Humble, Texas 77347
www.spiritscribepublishing.com
(832) 445-6229

Stampley Ministries, Inc.
1036 W. Atkinson Avenue
Milwaukee, Wisconsin 53206
Phone: (414) 534-4450
Website: stampleyministries.org
Email: stampleyministries@gmail.com

ISBN 978-0-692-86076-2

Parables of The Kingdom

(40 Lessons)

Nathaniel J. Stampley, Sr.

Parables of The Kingdom (40 Lessons)

Dr. Nathaniel J, Stampley Sr., Author

Printed in the United States of America
ISBN 978-0-692-86076-2

Contact Information:
Stampley Ministries Inc.
Milwaukee, Wisconsin 53206
www.stampleyministries.org
Email: stampleyministries@gmail.com
414-534-4450

Preface

I am not one who subscribes to a whole lot of attention and fan-fare because I prefer sharing more so than receiving. Nevertheless, I recognize Spiritual Gifts of Grace wherein blessings are bestowed upon us to pass them along. Therefore, on this spiritual journey, I have been blessed to embrace a few titles such as theologian, bishop, pastor, husband, father, grand-father (pa pa), missionary, ambassador, and Saint of the Most High God.

In 1967, I began my ministerial career in the Church of God in Christ in Baton Rouge, Louisiana (my birth-place). Since then, I have been blessed to serve as pastor in Lexington and Bay Springs, Mississippi; Baton Rouge, Louisiana; Dakar, Senegal, and Milwaukee, Wisconsin. During this journey as a preacher and teacher, I have gained wisdom and spiritual insights. Therefore, it is the lack of discipline and spiritual maturity among both the laity and leadership that inspires me to write this book.

For example, it appears far too many individuals in the Church have restricted his or her orientation exclusively to the literal (face value) approach of the Bible. While this approach is appropriate, it is equally important to embrace the critical approach (research/analysis) to the same. In doing so, the reader will appreciate the importance to wholesome study and experience balance, inspiration (literal), and information (critical).

Jesus Christ came with a spiritual mandate precisely proclaiming the *Gospel of the Kingdom* during an era when the masses experience political, economic, and religious oppression. The message of the kingdom is soul-stirring, prophetic, and liberating versus mere rituals, emotional outbursts, and fashionable clichés.

Initially, these lessons surfaced in 2006 during our weekly Bible Study Class on Thursday at Heritage International Ministries Church of God in Christ in Milwaukee, WI. I am the pastor of the church. Jesus utilized parables as a means of unlocking or revealing the mysteries of God. Therefore, this book is designed to assist laity and leadership within the faith as well as provide insights to those who stand outside the Church.

Table of Contents

Section 1

Critical and Literal Approach to Studying Parables

A mystery is something hidden and truth is the mystery revealed. Jesus Christ came to unlock the mysteries of God and this is expressed through the Life and Teachings of Jesus Christ. The prefix *Para* denotes beside. The suffix *Balleim* means "to throw." The term *Parabole* is a Greek word meaning "to place alongside a story in order to assist in attaining truth." Parables are insightful stories drawn from scenes of nature or common experiences in order to convey a truth. A parable is distinguished from a fable such as the story of *The Lion and The Elephant*. A fable is a fictitious story meant to teach a moral lesson and the characters are usually animals.

It warrants mentioning you should not try to make every detail in a parable relevant. The underlying message is more important than the illustrations contained in the stories. After all they are pointing to a unique aspect of the Kingdom of God.

Jesus was a Master Storyteller. He embraced an ancient-African-oratorical discipline and introduced the Kingdom of God, practically and colorfully. His withholding the meaning on the front-end from the masses (Matthew 13:34-35 & Mark 4:10-13) served as an act of divine judgment upon the unworthy and so-called religious authorities.

The Old and New Testaments point to the Kingdom of God being established on earth as a reflection of His eternal purpose. The Hebrew term *Malkut* and the Greek term *Basileia* refer to kingdom. Generally speaking, the scriptures refer to the Kingdom of God as the reign of spiritual authority on earth via the Believers in Christ. Furthermore, this kingdom is holy in nature and includes being territorial and eternal.

The Kingdom of God is grounded in Holiness, Righteous, Faith, and Love. There are three unique characters or titles associated with the Messianic Kingdom:

- *King* – Anointed Ruler or administer of justice and mercy; regal and royal. Authorized to teach the Law.

- *Priest* – Anointed official who mediates at the altar between the people and God, and teaches the Law.

- *Prophet* – Anointed messenger who declares the oracles of God unto the covenant community and beyond. They foretell the future, while at the same time; challenge the community to live righteously. Authorized to teach the Law.

The Kingdom of God is spiritual in nature and designed to expand perpetually. The New Testament gives us a mature perspective of God's eternal purpose for the Church on earth. Jesus used parables in order to disclose the hidden truths that the religious leaders were distorting. More parables are recorded in Luke than any of the other three Gospels.

Altogether, I have discovered 40 parables, while other researchers share less. Nevertheless, they are uniquely preserved in the Bible; whereby, they may help you understand the Gospel of the Kingdom and the mission of the Church as a *Called Out Assembly*. The foundation or key ingredients for parables stem from the following: maxims, metaphors, similes, Proverbs, and figures of speech. A parable is the expansion of a thought or word that is developed into a story. Ultimately, these colorful parables are found in the New Testament Synoptic Gospels: Matthew, Mark, and Luke. The Gospel according to John does record parables, but this is not to say he does not share stories. There are more parables recorded within the Synoptic Gospels (especially Luke) than the other two Gospels.

Viewing the Kingdom of God through the Eyes of Parables

Theological Perspective

Parables consist of hidden spiritual treasures that are housed in earthen vessels. Ethical, practical, and spiritual messages are conveyed through these stories. The stories have the unique ability to pique your interest and finally opening your heart and soul to an eternal message.

How does a parable usually appear in scripture?

Generally speaking Jesus utilized parables to address the following groups:

- **Multitude**

- **Religious Leaders**

- **Disciples**

In either case, He is showing them an aspect of the truth that was previously missed or distorted. Usually, the details in a parable give us the necessary background in order to make the story realistic, but they should not be taken point by point.

Why are parables so important, and why do we need to understand them?

There are various methods utilized by God to bring about reconciliation. Parables are effective tools, which help open our hearts and eyes to the spiritual deficiency at hand. Ignoring the truth is another way of demonstrating disobedience and arrogance to what Jesus had to say. Hearing and understanding is the gateway to experiencing a fulfilled life. Simply stated, parables inform and enable us to live righteously and overcome the adversities in a sinful world.

Format or study guide regarding each of the parables:

1. What are the circumstances surrounding the origin of the parable?

2. Who is the parable addressed to?

3. What is the subject drawn from? (Nature or common experience)

4. Look at the variations in the Synoptic Gospels.

5. What applications can we make for our lives?

6. Can you tell the story in your own words?

History and Examples of Parables in the Old Testament

In another publication called *Doctrines of the Church,* I stated, "in order to establish and teach sound Church Doctrines one must be orientated in the Old Testament." This statement holds true to the study of parables.

Storytelling is as old as man and woman emerging from the Motherland, Africa. The oral tradition is embedded in all cultures around the world simply because it is a creative way to preserve culture and pass along traditional values. Therefore, parables did not just occur during Jesus' ministry in the New Testament.

The Hebrew term *Mashal* refers to riddles or parables. It is also a comparison of familiar earthly things with a heavenly or spiritual truth that is to be understood. It is noted that there are no less than twenty-nine parables in the Old Testament. Plus, a few references that will assist you in seeing an Old Testament pattern carried over in the New Testament are listed below.

- The Poor Man's Lamb regarding the Prophet Nathan speaking to King David (2 Samuel 12:4)

- Two Fighting Brothers and the Avengers of Blood and the Wise Widow of Tekoa (2 Samuel 14:1-11)

- The Escaped Prisoner and a Prophet to King Ahab (1 Kings 20:35-40)

- The Fruitless Vineyard and Isaiah speaking to Israel and Judah (Isaiah 5:1-7)

- Two Eagles and the Vine when Ezekiel speaks to the House of Israel (Ezekiel 17:3-10)

- The Lioness and Cubs as Ezekiel speaks to House of Israel (Ezekiel 19:2-9)

- The Boiling Cauldron as Ezekiel speaks to House of Israel (Ezekiel 24:3-5)

- The Talking Donkey as Balaam is warned by the Angel (Numbers 22:28)

- The Potter and Clay wherein, Yahweh speaks to Jeremiah (Jeremiah 18:1-10)

- The Trees Making Kings when Abimelech slew his brothers (Judges 9:7-15)

- The Drunkard represents the counsel of Solomon (Proverbs 23:29-35)

- True and False Prophets reflect Ezekiel's Lament during the captivity (Zechariah 11:3-10)

- Dry Bones in the Valley recapture the vision of Ezekiel (Ezekiel 37:1-15)

Other scriptural references are noted in 2 Samuel 12:7 and Habakkuk 2:6. It should be observed that there appears to be more parables in Ezekiel than any other Old Testament Book.

40 Parables in the Synoptic Gospels

Matthew	Mark	Luke

1. Lamp under A Bushel

| 5:14-16 | 4:21-22 | 8:16-17 |

2. Wise and Foolish Builder

| 7:24-27 | | 6:47-49 |

3. New Cloth on an Old Garment

| 9:16 | 2:21 | 5:36 |

4. New Wine in Old Wineskins

| 9:17 | 2:22 | 5:37-38 |

5. The Sower

| 13: 2-23 | 4:2-20 | 8:4-15 |

6. The Tares (Weeds)

| 13:24-30 | | |

7. The Mustard Seed

| 13:31-32 | 4:30-32 | 13:18-19 |

8. The Leaven

| 13:33 | | 13:20-21 |

Matthew	Mark	Luke

9. The Hidden Treasurer

13:44

10. The Valuable Pearl

13:45-46

11. The Dragnet

13:47-50

12. The Lost Sheep

18:12-14   15:3-7

13. The Unforgiving Servant

18:23-35

14. The Workers in the Vineyard

20:1-16

15. The Two Sons

21:28-32

16. The Wicked Vinedresser

21:33-45   12:1-12   20:9-19

17. The Wedding Feast

22:2-14

Matthew	Mark	Luke

18. The Fig Tree

| 24:32-35 | 12:28-32 | 21:29-33 |

19. The Wise & Foolish Virgins

25:1-13

20. The Talents

25:14-30

21. The Growing Seed

| 4:26-29 | 4:26-29 | |

22. The Absent Householder

| | 13:33-37 | |

23. The Creditor & Two Debtors

| | | 7:41-43 |

24. The Good Samaritan

| | | 10:29-37 |

25. A Friend in Need

| | | 11:5-13 |

26. A Rich Fool

12:16-21

Matthew	Mark	Luke

27. The Watchful Servant

12:35-40

28. The Faithful & Evil Servant

12:42-48

29. The Barren Fig Tree

13: 6-9

30. The Lesson on Humility

14: 7-14

31. The Great Supper

14:16-24

**32. Building a Tower & King
   Making War**

14:25-35

33. The Lost Coin

15:8-10

34. The Lost Son

15:11-32

35. The Unjust Steward

16:1-13

Matthew	Mark	Luke

36. The Rich Man & Lazarus

16:19-31

37. The Unprofitable Servants

17:7-10

38. The Persistent Widow

18:1-8

39. **The Pharisees & Tax Collector**

18:9-14

40. **The Minas (Pounds)**

19:11-27

1. The Lamp under a Bushel
(Matthew 5:14-16; Mark 4:21-22 & Luke 8:16-17)

We are about to embark upon a spiritual journey that will help unlock the mysteries of the Kingdom of God. There are some schools of thought that omit this story as a parable and simply treat it as a metaphor. However, we will treat this account as a parable. Therefore, this marks the first parable within the Synoptic Gospels. The parable is found in all three gospel accounts.

Jesus shares a relatively short story pertaining to a lamp in a dark room. The term *bushel* is used interchangeably with a basket because both represent a container. We must also view our lives as the container of righteousness in a darken world that is filled with unrighteousness. This short illustration is profound because it conveys the importance of positioning yourself at all times to be a faithful witness for the Lord. There is yet another account in Luke 11:33-36.

1. What are the circumstances surrounding the origin of this parable?

- Matthew records this parable as part of the Sermon on the Mount (Chapters 5-7)

- Mark places Jesus by the Sea of Galilee teaching the Disciples (4:10-11) about the Kingdom of God.

- Luke describes Jesus teaching the masses as he travels to numerous towns in Galilee, and the disciples asks the meaning of the previous parable at some point (Luke 8:9-10).

2. Who is the parable addressed to?

In all three accounts, Jesus appears to be speaking to either the disciples or the multitude. However, it is appropriate to say all parables serve as spiritual indictments against the religious leaders.

3. What is the parable drawn from?

- The parable is drawn from a common experience (lamp)

- The New Testament Greek word *Lampas* denotes a torch or lantern. The term *Luchnos* refers to a lamp stand that is fueled by oil.

- The term oil is derived from *Elaion*. It refers to olive oil that has been beaten and symbolizes the Holy Spirit.

- The term *bushel* derives from the word *Modios*, a dry measure or container equivalent to a peck.

4. Variations in the Gospels

- This parable is located in all three gospels, and a few observations are listed below:

- Matthew begins by making reference to a light and a city on a hill. Both are distinct and should not be hidden. In addition, Matthew is the only one who shared three verses regarding this parable.

- Both Matthew and Mark refer to a lamp not being effective in the house if it was placed under a bushel or bed.

- Luke is the only one who used the term *vessel* (not *bushel*).

- Matthew and Luke are the only ones who give a commentary on the benefits of light throughout the house.

- Mark and Luke end with the same message - secrets will be manifested as a result of the light.

- Only Matthew ends by metaphorically reminding us of the good works emanating from the light of righteousness and giving glory to the Father.

5. What applications can we make for our lives?

Our daily experiences are filled with light and darkness, good and evil, and right and wrong. The parable of the lamp serves as a vivid reminder we must position and elevate ourselves, so that the radiance of His glory will shine through us. Have you ever seen someone display a beautifully expensive lamp in their home? However, that lamp was solely there for decoration because it did not work. In contrast, there are people with all sorts of temporal gadgets occupying his or her time, but they are not displaying the light of His glory. If the light (consciousness) is not shining in your life, it is a clear indication that sin has darkened your soul.

6. Can you tell the story in your own words?

Jesus shared an enlightening account regarding the role of light in a dark room. Darkness keeps us from seeing and moving in a precise manner. However, the lamp will make a world of difference upon being fueled with oil in it.

Our body represents the lamp and the city on the hill. The lamp is able to emit light simply because of the oil within it. Each of you is encouraged to allow the Holy Spirit (oil) to flow through you, so that you might be able to remove the darkness in and around you.

The light not only benefits the individual holding it, but it also benefits all those who come into the area. The light serves as a source of energy and confidence to move about without stumbling. Let us take the lamp and place it on the stand of holiness as opposed to being timid and withdrawn. Jesus is the Light of the World, and He has extended His source of light and life to permeate through our lives.

2. The Wise and Foolish Builders
(Matthew 7:24-27; Luke 6:47-49)

This parable is part of the *Sermon on the Mount/ Sermon on the Plain* delivered by Jesus in Galilee. In this parable, Jesus' teaching on the kingdom emphasizes the following: hearing the Word of God and doing what the Word declares.

To a large degree, people listen and receive vital information, but far too many of the same fail to adhere and obey. It is great to read or study the Bible, but it is equally important to practice its teaching on a daily basis.

1. What are the circumstances surrounding the origin of the parable?

- In Matthew, Jesus is teaching the multitude as part of the Sermon on the Mount.

- In Luke's account, Jesus is teaching the multitude and disciples as part of the Sermon on the Plain.

- In both cases, the parable serves as part of Jesus' initial teachings before a large crowd. These practical, ethical, and spiritual teachings are benchmarks and distinguish Jesus from the religious leaders.

2. Who is it addressed to?

In both gospel accounts, Jesus is speaking primarily to the crowd, but the disciples and religious leaders are also in the midst.

3. What is the subject drawn from?

The parable is drawn from a common experience (house), but elements of nature such as water and earth are utilized. The Hebrew term *Bayit* denotes house and an established dwelling place. The New Testament Greek term *Oikos* basically means the same. In addition, these terms may also refer to physical and spiritual dwelling places. All communities have need of constructing residences, so we must be careful and prudent where and how we build.

The natural elements and her diverse forms such as water, flood, rock, and sand may present challenges. Building a house on a rock will prove to be far better than building the same on the sand.

4. Variations in the gospels.

- In Matthew and Luke, we are encouraged to hear and obey divine instructions; therein, lies the opportunity to become wise.

- The house is used metaphorically for the way people live and behave in life.

- Matthew indicates the house was built upon a rock. Whereas, Luke indicates he dug deep into the rock prior to building the house.

- The rain came and resulted in flooding, but the house was able to withstand.

- In contrast, the other man received the same instruction, but chose to build his house, differently.

Matthew says he built his house on the sand. Luke indicates he built without a foundation.

- In both cases, the house was not able to withstand the same test, and eventually was destroyed.

5. What applications can we make for our lives?

It is important for each of you to listen and obey the Word of God. For example, I observe many adults involved in doing certain things such as smoking, using drugs, fornicating, using profanity, stealing and lying, etc. However, an adult will engage in some or all of the above. It is best to practice what you teach.

Another illustration is the way our nation tends to justify declaring war against another nation. Peace is greater than chaos, and there are no winners in war. Wisdom is a proven path to wholesome living. However, a life of foolishness will lead to death and destruction.

6. Can you tell the story in your own words?

There is a thin line between success and failure, hearing and doing, and truth and fallacy. Jesus used this parable to help unlock another mystery about the kingdom. The worldly orientation is tempting and lures you into taking short cuts in life. A physical structure must have an adequate foundation in order for it to survive diverse challenges. On the other hand, you must deposit the Word of God in your heart spiritually because challenges are inevitable. Be very careful where you build in life.

3. The New Cloth on Old Garments
(Matthew 9:16; Mark 2:21 & Luke 5:36)

This is a relatively short parable consisting of a single verse. Nevertheless, it is just as relevant. We are about to discover that the parable serves as a transition; wherein, John the Baptist is concluding his ministry. Moreover, Jesus Christ is launching his new ministry in Galilee.

Furthermore, we should keep in mind the *Old Way* fulfilled a purpose, but the *New Way* is equally important because she will usher in the Dispensation of Grace and the Kingdom of God.

1. What are the circumstances surrounding the origin of this parable?

- All three gospel accounts place Jesus in Capernaum (adopted home) ministering to the people.

- Jesus came upon Matthew (Levi), the tax collector, and summoned him to follow. Afterward, He goes to his home and fellowship.

- The Pharisees and Scribes take offense with Jesus mingling with publicans (ungodly Hebrews who engaged in tax collecting) and sinners.

- The disciples of John the Baptist and Pharisees customarily fasted. Therefore, someone wanted to know why Jesus' disciples were not fasting?

2. Who is it addressed to?

Jesus is responding to a question presented by John's disciples and religious leaders. However, He is also taking advantage of teaching the disciples and the multitude the truth about the Kingdom of God.

3. What is the subject drawn from?

- The parable is drawn from a common experience (cloth).

- The Old Testament Hebrew term *Labas* refers to clothes. The New Testament Greek terms *Himation & Amphienumi* denotes clothes, garments, fabric, and material. Generally speaking, garments are used for covering the body against the elements or used as a distinction in society. Metaphorically, garments can refer to spiritual or carnal concerns.

- In all three accounts, they indicate the garment will eventually wear out. Sometimes, you can sew or mend the garments, but they need to be replaced in other circumstances.

4. Variations in the gospels.

- Overall, this parable displays more consistency, but here are a few observations.

- Matthew states, "No one puts…"

- Mark states, "No one sews…"

- Luke states, "No one tears…"

- In each scenario, the reference is made wherein the new is trying to place a patch or repair something old and worn out.

5. What applications can we make for our lives?

It is very common to see activities and traditions in the church that is inappropriate, yet traditional. For example, denominations have played a significant role in the Church, but we must be very careful and not allow the *Spirit of Error* to outweigh the *Spirit of Truth.* I promote discipline and theological studies while remaining humble. We must never allow the spirit of the entitlement to influence us such as seen in the Scribes and Pharisees. Jesus Christ brought a refreshing and liberating approach to worship and service as opposed to self-righteousness and a legalistic approach to religion.

6. Can you tell the story in your own words?

Jesus was in the early stage of His ministry when the parable was told. He healed the sick, called a disciple, and fellowshipped with the unexpected. He continued disclosing insights regarding fasting. The religious leaders should have known better, but they became spiritual stumbling-blocks, instead.

Therefore, he seized the moment to help everyone understand He does not represent the status-quo as another Rabbi. Instead, He is the Son of God (new garment) and refused to be identified with self-righteousness (old garments). The gospel is welcoming and inclusive for to those who felt left out. Therefore, let us put on the newness in Christ.

4. New Wine in Old Skins
(Matthew 9:17; Mark 2:22 & Luke 5:37-38)

The parable follows the account of the New Cloth and Old Garments. It is also relatively short and gets to the point. In some schools of thought, this parable and the previous one is not treated, accordingly. However, we will come to discover Jesus utilized this illustration for drawing attention to the *changing of the guard* regarding the religious leaders inadequately representing the House of Israel and Kingdom of God.

The Old Way should not be viewed as something bad just like the Law should not be viewed in that manner. For example, John the Baptist and The Prophets represented the Old Way and were significant in declaring the oracles of God. Contrarily, the New Way is ushered in by the Dispensation of Grace. The parable is found in all the Synoptic Gospels.

1. What are the circumstances surrounding the origin of this parable?

- The circumstances are identical to the previous parable. Let me reiterate.

- In all three Gospels, Jesus had returned to Capernaum and was ministering.

- Jesus came upon Matthew (Levi), a tax collector and summoned Him to follow. Afterward, Jesus goes to his home and fellowship with others and him.

- The Pharisees and Scribes tool offense mingling with publicans and sinners.

- The disciples of John and Pharisees customarily fasted. Therefore, someone wanted to know why Jesus' disciples were not fasting.

2. Who is it addressed to?

Jesus is responding to a question asked by John's disciple and religious leaders. However, He is also taking advantage of teaching the disciples and the multitude aspects regarding the Kingdom of God.

3. What is the subject drawn from?

- The parable is drawn from a scene of nature.

- The Old Testament term *Yayim* and New Testament word *Oinos* refers to wine. Generally speaking, wine is derived from fermented grapes. Wine was commonly used during feasts and family gatherings.

- Metaphorically, wine is also used in scripture as the *Spirit.*

4. Variations in the gospels.

- All three accounts basically say the same thing. However, Luke records two verses.

- Placing new wine in old skin will cause the animal skin to burst.

- John the Baptist served faithfully, but Jesus cannot be like John.

5. What applications can we make for our lives?

The universal church has presented many wonderful and not so wonderful traditions. Jesus Christ represents the new nature or expression that is steeped in Grace. The old tradition tends to cause restrictions and finger-pointing. The Hebrew term *Hadas* refers to something new. The New Testament term *Kainos* denotes something recent, different, fresh and unique versus something that has already existed and lost its appeal. Each of you are encouraged to drink the new wine of the Holy Spirit with an open mind as opposed to Old Wine Skin habits that alienate us from God and each other.

6. Can you tell the story in your own words?

Jesus shared this brief story in a profound manner because it instructs us on how we should behave. Nostalgia has a place when it comes to righteous examples. John the Baptist will always be reverenced as an honorable prophet. Jesus Christ represented a fresh start and creative spirit who invited both Jews and Gentiles into the Kingdom of God. You cannot be effective in the ministry of reconciliation if you are stuck in the past. Christ represents liberty and transformation.

5. The Sower
(Matthew 13:3-23; Mark 4:2-20 & Luke 8:4-15)

This marks the 5th parable noted as the longest thus far. There is consistency in each of the stories because each adds to unlocking the mysteries of the kingdom. Keep in mind a parable is a story conveying spiritual, ethical, and practical truth. The central point in this parable permeates around understanding the sacredness of the seed (word). In addition, we must pay attention to the handler and conditions of the soil if we truly expect to have a productive harvest. It has been said, "When the conditions for growth are met, growth will occur."

1. What are the circumstances surrounding the origin of this parable?

It appears Jesus is in Galilee on a preaching tour. Furthermore, it is stated He is in a boat or standing by the sea teaching about the kingdom. Luke's account does not mention a boat.

2. Who is it addressed to?

Specifically speaking, Jesus is teaching the multitude. However, in a more profound way, He was also giving spiritual insights to the disciples. Lastly, his message serves as an indictment against religious leaders.

3. What is the subject drawn from?

The parable is drawn from a scene from nature, seed, and soil. Alternatively, it also reflects a common experience because of the role of the sower/farmer.

- The Old Testament term *Zara* refers to a scattered seed or to make pregnant. The term *Zera* is a noun denoting seedtime, harvest, offspring, descendant, and posterity.

- The New Testament term *Speiro* refers to planting a seed.

- Metaphorically and spiritually, it refers to making a deposit in the Kingdom of God.

- For the most part, Israel was associated with agriculture. Thus, the land, planting, cultivating, harvesting, and seasons played a significant role and this gave birth to a series of holy days.

4. Variations in the gospels.

- Each gospel account mentions the four categories of disbursing the seeds: *along the path, among the rocks, among the thorns, and in good ground.*

- Only Luke varies by mentioning growth that failed to occur due to a lack of moisture.

- In the 3rd scenario (thorn), each one gives a slight distinction of what happened and the outcome.

- In the 4th scenario (good ground), Matthew and Mark shares with us various potentials and outcomes: *Thirty-Fold, Sixty-Fold, & One Hundred-Fold.*

- Luke is the only one who refers to the One Hundred-Fold.

- Some land can produce at her maximum: thirty, sixty and one hundred percent, and so it is in life.

- Upon hearing the parable, some disciples approached Jesus and asked for an interpretation.

- Matthew refers to the prophet Isaiah (6:9-10)

- In the explanation, Matthew and Luke suggest the best place for the Word (seed) is the heart, which is your conscious core.

- Matthew and Mark shared thoughts regarding the thirty, sixty, and one hundred percent yield. Whereas, Luke mentioned the bringing forth of the good fruit.

5. What application can you make for our lives?

For all of those who are faithful disciples of Christ, you represent the Sower. The Word (sowed) is sacred, but it needs to be deposited in various ways day after day. Let me illustrate:

- Some people casually receive the Word every Sunday because it is customary and culturally polite to attend a congregation (along the way).

- Others engage in church traditions and rituals which often results in being self-righteous, void of God's grace (stony ground).

- Furthermore, there are those with good intentions and appear to have a sincere heart, but they are easily influenced and get persuaded to follow the wrong path until he or she discovers all the joy and love for Christ are choked out of them (thorns).

- A faithful witness of Christ will follow the teachings and help bring forth more fruit unto righteousness (good ground).

6. Can you tell the story in your own words?

I simply love the way Jesus presented samplings of the way people behave regarding spiritual concerns. Religious influence and persuasion comes across in many forms. However, I also see far too many people doing just enough to get by.

In all gospel accounts and scenarios, the Word or seed was accepted or deposited (so to speak). Being casual, haphazard, or nonchalant about matters of life will always come back and haunt you. The ultimate seed is Christ, and every good seed has a potential to germinate. However, be mindful of planting seeds in inappropriate places.

6. The Wheat and Tares
(Matthew 13:24-30; 37-43)

Comments

We are about to get acquainted with a parable that will help us understand another aspect of the Kingdom of God. More specifically, we will observe a separation between the followers of Christ (wheat) and the sinners (tares). A good farmer plants early and expects a good harvest. Furthermore, they can tell the difference in the *wheat & tares*, in a similar manner, like God can detect the true worshippers. This parable follows the parable of the Sower.

Perhaps this little story will help us appreciate the truth. The people who failed to tell the truth are likely to be exposed. The case of a country preacher who said to his congregation is one example:

"Folks, *Liars* is the subject of my sermon this evening. How many in the congregation has read the 69th chapter of Matthew?"

Nearly every hand in the congregation went up, immediately.

"That's right," said the pastor. "You're just the individuals I want to preach to. There is no 69th chapter in Matthew."

1. What were the circumstances surrounding the origin of this parable?

In the previous parable, we observe Jesus sitting in a boat on the Sea of Galilee, teaching a large crowd of believers regarding the Kingdom of God.

2. Who was Jesus addressing when He gave this parable?

Jesus was speaking specifically to the crowd that had gathered along the sea; however, the message also had relevance for the disciples and religious leaders.

3. What is the subject drawn from?

This parable utilizes scenes from nature (i.e. wheat and tares). For example, the Old Testament term *Chittah* and the New Testament term *Sito* refers to wheat, corn, or grain in scripture. Generally speaking, wheat is a cereal grass, and upon grounding it, bread and pasta are derivatives of it. Wheat in Kemit (Egypt) and Palestine (Canaan) have been altered due to agri-business. For further information regarding Genetically Modified Organisms (GMO), let me recommend the book, *Wheat Belly: A Total Health Plan* by Dr. William Davis.

Alternatively, the term tares stems from the New Testament Greek words *Lizarion* and *Darnel* that resemble wheat in appearance and grows along-side it. Tares are actually poisonous and wild, and the prudent farmer usually separates them at harvest. Metaphorically speaking, they are called *Bastards & Sons of the Evil One.* Therefore, beware of false fruits or seeds, being infiltrated within the Kingdom of God.

4. Look at the variations in the gospel.

This parable is only recorded in Matthew. Nonetheless, let me share a few highlights.

- The good and bad seeds (verses 24-27)

- Separation of the wheat and tares (verses 20-30)

- Explanation & symbols of good and evil (verses 37-39)

- The separation/judgment (verses 40-43)

5. What applications can we make for our lives?

The good seed is the Word of God (Jesus) planted in the heart of a believer. Meanwhile, Satan (tares) is the master of sneaking in and disguising himself alongside the good seeds. We must guard ourselves against carnality, pride, traditions, philosophies and materialism. Quite often I hear people in the Church suggesting we ought to get rid of or remove certain persons within the congregation, due to their misbehaving. However, we must be very careful and sometime allow certain things to run its course until the harvest (return of Christ). After all, Jesus allowed Judas to remain a disciple until the very end. There is a profound lesson in discipline and humility for the saints to remain focused.

6. Can you tell the story in your own words?

Jesus masterfully illustrated how a good deed became challenged or infiltrated by a bad deed. Bad things can and will happen to good people, but the truth will prevail in the end. Jesus gave us a detailed account i.e. while planting good seeds. Bad seeds are mixed with the good ones while the servant is asleep. Householder is not disturbed about this bad deed. There is divine wisdom in realizing and allowing the wheat and tares to grow, together. The wheat will ultimately be gathered into the storehouse, but the tares will be bundled up and burned. In the end, Jesus admonished the listeners to hear and take heed to the parable.

7. The Mustard Seed
(Matthew 13:31-32; Mark 4:30-32; Luke 13:18-19)

Comments

This marks the 7th parable Jesus preserved in the Gospels. It is also, the 3rd parable in the 13th chapter of Matthew. We should never lose sight of these colorful stories that hinges upon Jesus shedding light or giving insights into the *Kingdom of God/Heaven*. For the most part, people living in the United States of America have a different perspective of *Mustard Seeds* than what we will study in the text. Nonetheless, in all cases, a mustard seed is minute in size, but has the potential to expand into an enormous tree.

1. What are the circumstances surrounding the origin of this parable?

This parable comes immediately after the Parable of the Wheat and Tares, and its origin permeates around the same situation mentioned in Matthew and Mark. However, in Luke's account, it follows the classic story of Jesus healing the *woman with the issue of blood* following eighteen years of misery.

2. Who was Jesus addressing when He gave the parable?

Just like the previous parables of this chapter, He is speaking to the crowd. However, it has significance to the disciples and religious leaders.

3. What is the subject drawn from?

This parable is drawn from a scene in nature called the *Mustard Seed.* The New Testament Greek term *Sinapi* derives from Egypt, and denotes mustard seed. It is a Eurasian plant with a tiny seed, but emerges into a very large tree with branches reaching ten to twelve feet in height. They are known to be a favorite resting spot for birds.

4. Look at variations in the parables.

- Both Mark and Luke begin the parable by asking a question.

- Matthew introduces the parable by making a declaration about the Kingdom.

- All 3 accounts refer to the seed being planted in the following manner: *in the field* (Matthew); *in the ground* (Mark); *in the garden* (Luke).

- Once the seed is planted it *becomes the greatest of plants/trees* (Matthew); *largest of all garden plants and produces large branches* (Mark); *grew into a tree* (Luke).

- *Birds came and made nests* (Matthew); *birds made nests in the shade* (Mark); *birds of the air made nests in its branches* (Luke).

All in all, there are minimal variations in these parables.

5. What applications can we make for our lives?

The mustard seed is a powerful illustration of potentiality. Quite often, I see people in the Church who should know better, yet they allow circumstances to overwhelm or discourage them resulting in a stunted growth in faith. There is truth in these axioms, which says, "Big things come in small packages," and "Bite by bite the ants will eat the elephant."

6. Can you tell the story in your own words?

The truth is revealing or a discovery that has been hidden. Jesus masterfully showed how a simple seed, taken by a person, is deposited into a welcoming soil and eventually becomes enormous in size. Likewise, every believer in Christ is expected to grow in grace and knowledge. The result of the tree is connected to her humble origin as a small seed. Therefore, faith is the link to stable growth. *If a little tree grows in the shadow of a big tree, then it will die.* I want to encourage you to look within and not without, so that you too will reach your fullest potential within the Kingdom of God.

8. The Leaven
(Matthew 13:33 and Luke 13:20-21)
Comments

This is the 8th parable shared by Jesus as it relates to the Kingdom of God. It is relatively short and precise. Something I cannot emphasize enough is allowing the story to speak about the issue at hand and do not try to make it larger than life.

This parable serves as an indictment against the religious leaders (Pharisees & Sadducees) because they were not spiritually aligned to recognize Jesus Christ.

1. What were the circumstances surrounding the origin of this parable?

- In Matthew's account, Jesus is teaching the multitude about the Kingdom of God along the Sea of Galilee as observed in the preceding parable?

- In Luke's account, it appears Jesus is teaching and healing on the Sabbath Day in a synagogue.

2. Who is the parable addressed to?

In both gospels it appears Jesus is teaching the masses about the Kingdom of God. However, you can also apply the message has reference for the religious leaders who were standing nearby.

3. What is the subject drawn from?

This subject is drawn from nature. There are many references in scripture pertaining to leaven. The New Testament Greek term *Zume* references to leaven. Now, it is dough in a high state of fermentation that is used for baking bread. It was a slow process where yeast or leaven was known to multiply quietly and penetrate the other ingredients in the bread upon being applied. Eventually, the bread would slowly rise or transform the product into something other than its present form.

4. Variations in the gospel.

It appears both Matthew and Luke accounts utilized the same source. Furthermore, they make it clear the lesser (leaven) seems to have influence or penetrating power over the greater (mean) and ultimately makes an impact.

5. What applications can we make for our lives?

In many instances, the Bible seems to refer to leaven in a negative way or as a symbol of evil. Yes, evil can influence and corrupt in a similar manner as the leaven. However, Jesus seems to be utilizing this parable by inferring the righteous can make a powerful impact within their environment (like the leaven). You can look at a glass and call it half empty or half full.

6. Can you tell the story in your own words?

Jesus is making it clear the Word of God is similar to leaven, and this suggest a penetrating spirit will transform the lives of all those who come in contact with her. The Word of God is active and outweighs any negative element in her path. Therefore, if we are faithful and genuine in our witnessing, we will see a glorious manifestation of the power of God all around us.

Now, on the other hand, let us assume the leaven was used in this parable in a negative or evil fashion targeting the religious leaders. If so, we will see corruption and a misrepresentation of the truth distorting the lives of people. Evil serves as an opportunity for the righteous to stand up within the Kingdom of God. Leaven in bread will penetrate all ingredients just like poison in the bloodstream. We must remember it is the small things that operate behind the scenes that will ultimately corrupt you. "The basis of truth is within and not without." (Thurman). Jesus continued to teach in parables because the keys lie therein or spiritual treasures hidden from the proud and arrogant.

9. The Hidden Treasure
(Matthew 13:44)

Comments

This is the ninth parable of Jesus pertaining to the Kingdom of God. It is also the fifth parable found in the 13th chapter of Matthew. Remember parables are witty sayings that are usually expanded into a story. These stories are drawn from everyday realities.

In this particular parable, Jesus shares a brief story about the Kingdom of God by comparing it to a treasure hidden in a field. A whole lot of people like to think of the man that found the treasure as lucky. However, I would like to refer to him as a man on a spiritual journey who was ultimately rewarded.

1. What are the circumstances surrounding the origin of this parable?

It appears Jesus has left the crowd and entered a house.

2. Who is the parable addressed to?

- Jesus is speaking directly to the disciples.

- However, his teachings serve as an indictment on the religious leaders and instructions for the disciples.

3. What is the subject drawn from?

- I believe it is best to describe it as a scene from nature due to the treasure found in the field.

- The New Testament Greek term *thesaurus* refers to a valuable commodity stored away or hidden. Metaphorically, it refers to the heart being the depository of truth.

4. Variations of the Gospel.

- This parable is only found in Matthew.

- It appears Jesus is suggesting a certain man was blessed to find something very valuable i.e., gold, silver, onyx, etc. on a piece of property that was obviously for sale.

- The man knew the value of the treasure outweighed the purchase of the property.

- Spiritually, we must take the eternal message of truth contained in the Gospel and respond in a similar manner by wholeheartedly giving up whatever it takes to receive the ultimate yield in the Kingdom.

5. What applications can we make for our lives?

It appears far too many people come across great opportunities and fail to do what is necessary to seize it and expound upon it. Let us suppose you found an abandoned, antique piece of furniture or property near the interstate. At a first glance, it may not look appealing, but it can be rewarding later on in life if you secure it today. Or let us suppose, you discover oil or other minerals on a piece of property you want to buy. Would you disclose the secret or keep it to yourself? Perhaps, these are ethical dilemmas you will face, but valuable treasures in life must be kept a secret until the appropriate time in the final analysis. Once you are blessed and cultivate the findings, then you are in a better position to disclose and help others.

6. Can you tell the story in your own words?

Jesus drives home the point we should give up everything it takes to obtain the gift of salvation. There are various ways we can come into the Kingdom of God, but nothing happens by accident. God has strategically placed natural and spiritual treasures for you to discover. Upon knowing the truth, it is imperative for you to make the appropriate sacrifice to live in the Kingdom of God. The man in the story is not named, but his actions speak louder than words. He is presented as a model steward. If you walk in the spirit, then you will also come upon the hidden treasure, so that you can move on to the next level. Be patient in life, but act prudently as the doors of opportunity open for you.

10. The Pearl of Great Value
(Matthew 13:45-46)

Comment:

Once again, we are introduced to a simple parable pertaining to a *pearl* found only in the Gospel of Matthew. The Kingdom of God/Heaven is all about claiming territory and demonstrating spiritual authority. This marks the sixth parable in a series of nine disclosed in the same chapter. For all practical purposes, this parable is almost identical in style and format to the previous one (Hidden Treasure) with the exception of the circumstances.

1. What are the circumstances surrounding the origin of this parable?

It appears Jesus had concluded teaching the multitude along the Sea of Galilee (verse 36), and now he is about to give more insight into the kingdom by utilizing another parable.

2. Who is it addressed to?

Jesus is speaking specifically to the disciples. However, there are implications for the religious leaders nearby and who were mishandling the Word of God.

3. What is the subject drawn from?

I believe we can safely say this parable is drawn from both nature and common experience. For example, societies around the world, especially the Orient, have placed an esteemed value on *pearls.* Scripturally speaking, the New Testament term *Margarites* is used figuratively as something that is priceless. However, everyone does not possess the same value in judgment. Generally speaking, the pearl is found in the mouth of an oyster. A natural pearl is a smooth rounded bead formed within the shells of oysters and other mollusks (invertebrate marine creatures with a shell). In addition, pearls are organic gems created when an oyster covers a foreign object with beautiful outer layers of an iridescent coating called nacre, which is strong and resilient.

4. Variations in the Gospel.

This parable is found only in Matthew. Nonetheless, this parable introduces a man on a mission, wherein this discovery changes his socio-economic status in the community.

5. What applications can we make for our lives?

- A pearl is always hidden and so are the valuable things in life.

- A merchant is diligently searching for an expensive pearl.

- Upon finding the pearl, he keeps the value of it to himself.

- Afterwards, he sells everything in order to obtain this valuable commodity.

6. Can you tell the story in your own words?

This parable discloses tremendous spiritual benefits hidden within the Church; however, we should not take every detail verbatim.

- It is part of God's nature to plant and hide riches within the Kingdom of God.

- We must safeguard the priceless Word of God by depositing the same in the sacred chambers of our heart.

- In many cases, you are better off keeping some discoveries to yourself.

- We must learn how to position ourselves, whereby prosperity may be ascertained.

- There is truth in the African Proverb, "No one tells all they know."

This parable varies somewhat from the previous one. In this case, the man was deliberately searching for those gems. Apparently, someone other than himself already claimed ownership of the pearls (Jesus Christ) that had been gathered from the sea. We must also manage our time in such a way, so that our godly efforts will reward us with the treasures of life. "Usually, when God calls man, they are busy doing something" (African Proverb). Get busy and begin the search for the good things hidden in the Kingdom of God. We represent the merchant, and the pearl represents Christ. However, they are both within the Kingdom of God.

11. The Dragnet
(Matthew 13:47-50)

Comments

This is the 11th parable Jesus shared pertaining to the Kingdom of God. This will also signal the final parable in Chapter 13. Jesus utilized parables as a principle means of unlocking the mysteries of the Kingdom of God. This parable differs from the previous two simply because, after sharing the parable, Jesus indicates there will be judgment administered to those who fail to take heed to His teachings. He goes on to disclose a comparison with catching a fish being likened unto people.

1. What are the circumstances surrounding the origin of this parable?

Jesus is in a house near the Sea of Galilee, and he seizes the moment to make certain the disciples are clear on His teachings.

2. Who is the parable addressed to?

In verse 36, we observe Jesus directing his comments to the disciples. However, the parable has implications for the religious leaders and the multitude nearby.

3. What is the subject drawn from?

I believe the parable is drawn from a common experience. During Jesus' era, fishing was a very common trade and served as a major industry in Israel. The New

Testament term *net* stems from several Greek words. For example, *Sagene* refers to a dragnet.

- Fisherman had two basic modes of catching fish in large quantities.

- They could let the nets down into the water, draw them together in a narrow circle, and pull them into the boat.

- Alternatively, they would form a semicircle and draw the net to the shore. I believe this is the approach mentioned in our text (verse 48).

- A catch of fresh fish addressed both the personal and commercial needs of the community.

4. Variations in the Gospel.

- This parable is only found in Matthew.

- The journey through life is compared to a collection of fish. For example, in every community, people are presented with a variety of personalities, but in the end Christ will select those who are humble and fitted for the Kingdom.

5. What applications can we make for our lives?

Everyone should be cognizant of living responsibly in the *Dispensation of Grace* because that indicates we are in the last days. Satan is the master of disguise and deception. The judgment represents a time of rewarding the faithful and punishing the faithless.

Naturally, there are some fish you can eat, while others should not be eaten. God has set a righteous standard, whereby Jesus Christ is the spiritual barometer for measuring our conduct. This judgment will not only be punitive, but it will also be permanent. Each of you represent a fish in the midst of a large catch. The pure or genuine heart will determine if you will be received or rejected in the Kingdom of God.

6. Can you tell the story in your own words?

Jesus seized the opportunity to instruct the disciples on how it will be at the close of the ages. All sorts of fish swim the sea, and so it is in the course of life. Both saints and sinners occupy the same territory on a daily basis. However, there is a day of reckoning in which no one knows when it will occur but the Lord. The fire and furnace represent a prepared place that is inescapable for the unrighteous. Therefore, a good fisherman knows which fish is acceptable and non-acceptable. Likewise, Christ is always extending his salvation for you to enter the eternal Kingdom of God.

12. The Lost Sheep
(Matthew 18:12-14 & Luke 15:3-7)
Comments

This is the 12th parable shared by Jesus. In both the Old and New Testaments, there are many profound illustrations about the relationship between the shepherd and sheep. This unique bond in scripture serves as an archetype between the finite and the infinite. If you grasp the significance of the of the shepherd's love for the sheep, you will begin to see even more of how much God loves and protects the flock. Despite the protection and care by the shepherd, sometimes the sheep will wander and go astray due to curiosity. Once the separation occurs, the sheep is likely to face adversaries, but this is also an opportunity for the *Shepherd* of our souls, Jesus Christ, to rescue us.

1. What are the circumstances surrounding the origin of this parable?

In both gospel accounts, Jesus is teaching in Galilee. Matthew places Jesus teaching about humility. Therefore, in order to really get the message across, He calls a little child standing nearby. Afterwards, Jesus shares the story about the sheep that went astray. However, in Luke's account, the parable is the second in a series of three. The whole notion of being lost or detached from the fold must become a priority for the shepherd.

2. Who is the parable addressed to?

In Matthew, Jesus was asked a question by the disciples pertaining to the greatest in the Kingdom of Heaven. However, in Luke, Jesus is being challenged by the religious leaders due to his interaction with tax collectors.

3. What is the subject drawn from?

The parable is drawn from both nature and a common experience. For example, shepherds (common experience) were very common during Jesus' ministry.

- The Hebrew term *Raah* and Greek term *Poimen* refers to shepherd. In essence, they supervise or manage domesticated animals by guiding and defending them. Metaphorically, they are spiritual leaders of the *Flock of God.*

- On the other hand, the term *sheep* (nature) stems from the Greek word *Probaton.* They were domesticated animals that display loyalty to the shepherd. They provided food, clothing, and maintenance of the field. Most importantly, they are usually seen with the shepherd.

4. Variations in the Gospel.

- Matthew's account presents an insightful message to the disciples, wherein they should adopt a new perspective on who is greatest in the kingdom. For Jesus, greatness is grounded in humility.

- Reference to 100 sheep represents God's *Election of Grace* or *Children of Promise.*

- In this account, we find the sheep in the mountain.

- Luke seems to focus on religious leaders' lack of representing the Kingdom of God.

- Once again, Jesus shares what is most important.

- In this parable, the sheep are in the wilderness.

5. What application can we make for our lives?

- There are profound lessons contained in the sheep-shepherd relationship.

- The 100 sheep represent a small entrepreneur who took great pride in keeping the flock together at all costs.

- Curiosity caused one sheep to go away.

- A sheep separated from the flock is in a dangerous situation.

- The lost sheep represented the spiritual state of Israel. Furthermore, the religious leaders were contributing to this unfortunate reality.

- The sheep chose to go astray, and the shepherd chose to go after the single sheep.

- The shepherd had the experience, compassion, and wherewithal to find the sheep.

- Upon finding the sheep, the shepherd was very happy to discover him safe. Afterwards, the shepherd demonstrates his love by placing the sheep on his shoulder and returning to the flock with him (restoration).

- Upon returning home, the shepherd did not punish the sheep, but allowed him to return to his natural environment with the flock.

- We cannot afford to allow one sheep or member of the faith community to go astray, and that is why the shepherd left the ninety-nine.

- There is strength and safety in unity (*Bolla Moi Dollay*- together is power) as reflected in this Senegalese saying.

6. Can you tell the story in your own words?

The whole notion of being lost or detached from your rightful place is an unwelcome feeling. This story helps shed light on our curiosity and being lured away. The parable goes on to show without being judgmental or punitive Jesus retrieves the lost sheep and returns the same to the sheep-fold. Sons and daughters of the Most High God have the same capacity to carry out the love and concern for those who have temporarily opted to go astray. Make sure you have done your part in going after and assisting those who are in harm's way and the grace of God will do the rest. Jesus gives us a profound lesson regarding lost and found. Being lost is a vulnerable state of being that alienates and detaches one from God. The ultimate course for this reality is destruction. A lion, wolf, bear, or other beasts cannot and will not attack an entire flock. However, they will wait patiently for the right moment to seize the isolated prey. There is safety and nourishment within the flock. Sometimes, things may look better or enticing outside the *Spirit of Truth*, but I urge you to stay with God. If you happen to go astray, please do not refuse the help from the *Shepherd* upon its offer.

13. The Unforgiving Servant
(Matthew 18:23-35)

Comments

Parables are colorful and analogous stories that give us insights into the Kingdom of God/Heaven. This parable discloses details about the way a legal debt was handled and mishandled both according to the *Law* and *Grace*. Jesus wants to stress the importance of legality, forgiveness, and kindness. This parable is found only in the book of Matthew.

1. What are the circumstances surrounding the origin of this parable?

Peter seems to be the unofficial spokesman for the disciples. Therefore, he is the puzzled about the principle surrounding forgiveness (Genesis 4:24). Biblically, the number seven refers to *completion/maturity* and was considered an esteemed number. However, the rabbi was teaching if someone offends you, forgive them three times and that should be sufficient. Therefore, Jesus steps forward to remove the limitation and clarify this issue with disciples as well as the religious authorities.

2. Who is the parable addressed to?

Jesus is responding to a direct question from Peter. However, this parable is applicable to the religious leaders and the masses near them.

3. What is the subject drawn from?

This parable permeates around a common experience. Indebtedness seems to be a consistent reality throughout all times and in all societies around the world:

- People usually want things even though they do not have means to settle the account.

- When a debt is incurred, it involves two parties: a lender and a borrower.

- To owe someone is an indication of trust or leniency which has been established in a transaction for an agreed period of time (Nehemiah 5:4-5).

- There have always been Biblical guidelines for borrowing and paying.

- Furthermore, there have always been laws for handling unpaid debts when due. This parable gives us two distinct types of debts and two different ways they were handled.

- Ultimately, it is best to apply divine mercy and judgment when a matter is mishandled.

4. Variations in the Gospels.

- The parable is found in Luke.

- The story is told of a king who summoned his servants to settle their accounts.

- One owed 10,000 talents (enormous amount of money) and his inability to pay resulted in being sold along with his wife, children, and all he owned.

- The servant pleaded for mercy, and the Master was moved by compassion and released him and forgave the debt.

- Meanwhile, the same man left and confronted someone who owed him far less, 100 denarii (approximately, $12,000.00).

- The man was unable to pay the debt just as he was unable to do, earlier.

- Instead of showing mercy, he choked and abused the man and demanded immediate payment.

- He asked for mercy and promised to pay, but instead placed him in prison.

- Someone observed this inappropriate behavior and told the Master what occurred.

- Upon hearing this he was upset, disappointed, and summoned him to return.

- The Master reminded him how merciful he was to him and how outrageously he behaved.

- Afterwards, he demanded this man be put in jail until all his debt was paid.

- Of course, being incarcerated lessened the opportunity to resolve the debt.

- God sees all you do, so it is best to apply mercy in legal situations such as debts.

5. What application can you make for our lives?

It is not unusual to want things that you cannot pay in full at the moment. It is best to live within your means while realizing once you enter a debt it is a legal obligation that you may or may not be relieved of. The story goes on to illustrate powerful men can also demonstrate compassion, while those of lesser rank in society can abuse. There are resounding benefits associated with forgiveness. However, the man and woman that fail to travel that road will ultimately learn a painful lesson in life, such as we see in this story.

6. Can you tell the story in your own words?

The parable gives a clear comparison the way it is in life. There are kind-hearted people and there are callous people. The man that did what was appropriate was blessed and the man who tried to manipulate was caught in his own web.

14. The Workers in the Vineyard
(Matthew 20:1-16)

Comments

Let me introduce you to the fourteenth parable Jesus shared with us about the Kingdom of God. We will soon find this parable reveals a unique approach to the manner in which agreements and compensations are handled in the Kingdom of God. In addition, we should take note there is a continuous need for laborers up until the last hour prior to the return of the householder/lord. Some schools of thought label this parable as the *Generous Employer*. Please pay close attention to the terms and agreement between the laborers and the employer.

1. What are the circumstances surrounding the origin of this parable?

It appears Jesus has left Galilee (Matthew 19:1) and entered the coast of Judea beyond the Jordan River. He is engaged in a series of conversations and acts of deliverance.

2. Who is this parable addressed to?

Based upon the latter verse in chapter 19, we can assume Jesus is speaking specifically to the disciples (see verse 23). However, there were others nearby listening to his teachings.

3. What is the subject drawn from?

- In this instance, Jesus draws from a common experience. However, when referring to the vineyard, it includes a scene from nature.

- The term *Householder* is a New Testament Greek word *oikodespotes* and it denotes the *master/head* of a house or sometimes called the *Goodman*.

- The term *vineyard*, an Old Testament term *kerem* refers to grapes growing along the slopes. Metaphorically, Israel and the Church are referred to as the vineyard.

- The term *laborer* a New Testament term *ergates* denotes working or a helper performing a task on behalf of an owner or master.

4. Variations in Gospels.

- This parable is found only in Matthew.

- We will observe the Householder going to the market place, seeking laborers five times: 6:00 a.m., 9:00 a.m., 12:00 p.m., 3:00 p.m. and 5:00 p.m. throughout the day.

- The living bible suggests each laborer agreed upon $20.00 wages from the Householder.

- Interestingly, the agreements remained a secret between each laborer and the Householder until the end of the day. Nonetheless, everyone received equal pay.

- God is fair and His compensating plan is inclusive for everyone who accepts the great invitation.

- At the end of the day, disbursements were made according to the terms and agreements established at the time of hiring the laborers.

- During the disbursements, the laborers who worked longer obviously felt entitled to more than those who worked one or three hours.

- Eventually, the Householder had to remind the disgruntled laborers about the agreements they made with him. Furthermore, the original laborers' agreements had nothing to do with the latter laborers.

5. What applications can we make for our lives?

There will always be a need for a work pool in order to address the needs on hand. Each of us should be grateful for the doors God opens without becoming envious and jealous about the opportunities afforded others. In a western oriented value system, the dollar and seniority seems to be paramount. Furthermore, there seems to be too much emphasis on seniority and a diverse pay scale rather than being grateful for the portion God has given each of us.

6. Can you tell the story in your own words?

Once again, Jesus masterfully disclosed the unique qualities inherent in the Kingdom of God through this parable. If only we would allow God to do the judging and rewarding, then we would broaden our spiritual perspective on God and each other. The world we live in pays too much attention to personal needs while downplaying the inclusive nature expressed in the Kingdom of God. Please pay close attention to spiritual benefits afforded you without worrying about the same compensation plan extended to others.

15. The Two Sons
(Matthew 21:28-32)

Comments

According to our calculations, this is the 15th parable in the Gospel. I cannot emphasize enough the parables serve as spiritual barometers for measuring what is spiritually and ethically correct as it relates to the Kingdom of God. Please do not lose sight of the truth conveyed while you are enjoying the story being told.

In this particular parable, Jesus seizes the moment to share a profound lesson about a request being made regarding a work assignment administered by a father and two responses by his sons. The text goes on to disclose the diverse nature of people; some will say one thing and end up doing otherwise. Alternatively, others will promise to do what is appropriate but fail to carry it out.

1. What are the circumstances surrounding the origin of this parable?

Jesus is approaching the end of his earthly ministry. Therefore, this placed him in Jerusalem at the temple engaged in a conversation with the religious leaders. More specifically, they wanted to know who sanctioned or authorized Him to teach on religious matters.

2. Who is the parable addressed to?

It appears Jesus is responding to the religious leaders, namely, the Chief Priest and Elders (21:23). However, these teachings have resounding benefits for the disciples and multitude.

3. What is the subject drawn from?

The parable is drawn from a common experience regarding family concerns.

4. Variations in the Gospels.

- Matthew is the only one who records this parable.

- The question is raised regarding authority; therefore, the Greek term *Exousia* denotes lawful power or judicial decision. In addition, it refers to jurisdiction, liberty and strength.

- The man with two sons may or may not have been wealthy, but the parable represents diversity or choices we often make in life.

- Work was needed in the vineyard. The terms for vineyard in Hebrew are *Kerem* and Greek is *Ampelon.* They basically refer to grapes grown on a slope and low-lying hill country.

- The first son initially refused to work, but he recognized his mistake and repented, later. The Hebrew term *Naham* has to do with change of mind, purpose, or heart. The noun *Metanoia* refers to after-thought. The son who initially refused soon realized this was inappropriate and ended up working.

- Afterwards, the father approached the second son regarding the same workload.

- This son immediately said yes, but this favorable response failed to produce work.

- Jesus asked the question, "Which of the two did the will of his father?"

- The religious leaders answered correctly by saying, "The first."

- Upon getting their attention and response, Jesus connected this story (1st son) with the tax collectors and harlots' change of heart, which allowed them also to enter the Kingdom of God instead of the religious leaders (2nd son) who appeared to be representing righteousness.

- Jesus reiterates the name, John the Baptist (21:25), in relation to righteousness as a means of demonstrating how the religious leaders clearly rejected Him. However, the sinners (tax collectors and harlots) repented and entered the Kingdom of God.

5. What applications can we make for our lives?

We live in a world that seems quick to place labels or categorize people. Quite often, those who think they know end up indicating they did not what they claimed. It is very important each of you be careful what you say, especially when it comes to spiritual concerns. There are many procrastinators and hypocrites around the Church occupying important space. The American African Community desperately needs workers and not talkers. We need people who will roll up his and her sleeves, remain true to what they promise and help make a difference.

6. Can you tell the story in your own words?

This story helps us see clearly the diversity in individuals. It is obvious there will be people amongst us with shortcomings and character deficiencies. On the other hand, there are those who display a *holier than thou* character and act as if they are *the gatekeepers to heaven.* Jesus makes it abundantly clear, it is far better to initially refuse or turn down the *great invitation* and then realize what you have done than to say you are spiritually on board but never produce fruits of righteousness. When the call to worship and service is extended, it is best to always be humble and say, "Yes Lord, I'll go." Life is filled with diversity, and the higher calling is also being made. What will your response be when the Lord comes to you?

16. The Wicked Vinedresser
(Matthew 21:33-45; Mark 12:1-12; Luke 20:9-19)

Comments

This is the 16th parable and is relatively lengthy. Once again, we are about to unlock another mystery pertaining to the Kingdom of God. During Jesus' lifetime, farming was very common. We are about to explore the role of the *Householder, Vinedresser/Husbandman, Servant* and *Son.*

There will always be a need for food, and that is precisely why planting takes place. However, a problem seems to arise when the time for harvesting and distributing occurs. All three of the Synoptic Gospels record this parable, so it is imperative for each of you to understand symbolism hidden beneath this story. The *Vinedresser/Husbandman* represents the religious and civil leaders in Israel. They were expected to lead the covenant community along a righteous path, but instead they were corrupt. The owner (Elohim) allowed the crops to be planted and put in a place along with a defensive plan to safeguard this investment until the harvest season. However, we will discover the greed and misrepresentation of those who were commissioned to oversee all aspects of the crops.

1. What are the circumstances surrounding the origin of this parable?

In all three accounts, Jesus is in Jerusalem because He is trying to expose the unrighteousness in the *House of Israel,* while at the same time usher in the Church just before His crucifixion.

2. Who is the parable addressed to?

In all three accounts, Jesus is dialoging with the chief priest, scribes, and elders in the temple because they asked Him, "By, what authority is he able to teach, preach, and heal?"

3. What is the subject drawn from?

Once again, let me remind you parables are drawn from common experiences or scenes of nature. In this parable, it seems as if it is drawn from both. For example, the vineyard represents a scene from nature, whereas the various characters reflect common experiences.

Now, let us share a few thoughts about the various scenes and titles within the parable.

- Householder – The New Testament Greek word *Oikos* has to do with a house, and the term *Despotes* refers to a master. Therefore, *Oikodespotes* has to do with the master of the house.

- Vineyard – The Old Testament Hebrew term *Kerem* refers to the place of planting and harvesting the grapes. Metaphorically speaking, it refers to

Israel's relationship with Yahweh (Psalms 80-1-15 & Isaiah 5:1-7).

- Vinedresser/Tenants – The New Testament term *Ampelourgos* refers to a worker in the vineyard.

- Servants – The Old Testament term *Sarat* and New Testament word *Doulos* denotes one that works or ministers on behalf of someone in authority.

- Hedged – The New Testament term *Phragmos* refers to a fence, paling, or wall. Symbolically, there was a partition between the Jews and Gentiles.

- Tower – The Old Testament term *Migdal* has to do with a small fortress, watch-tower, or podium.

- Winepress – The New Testament term *Lenos* served as a trough or vat for treading upon the grapes.

4. Variation in the Gospels.

- Both Matthew and Mark give a similar account in the opening verse; however, Luke leaves out the terms *householder, hedge, winepress*, and tower.

- Only Matthew uses the term *householder*.

- All three accounts indicate the servant came to gather fruit on behalf of the householder. However, Luke and Mark mentioned the servants were beaten and sent away empty-handed.

- Matthew shares more details pertaining to the outcome. For example, one servant was beaten, another killed and the last one stoned (Matthew 21:35).

- The householder is determined to benefit from the harvest; therefore, he sent another delegation. Matthew basically said the tenants repeated their actions. Mark gives a similar report to the one found in Matthew's initial report such as beating and killing the servants. Luke summarized it by saying they beat and treated the servants shamefully, but in the final analysis they too left empty-handed.

- In the third and final attempt, we observed the householder sending his only son to retrieve some of the harvest.

- All three accounts basically give the same scenario about the way they disrespected and killed the servant because they were under the erroneous assumption they could gain his inheritance.

- After this cruel act, each writer raised the question regarding what will the owner do to these tenants? Of course, they would receive the severest punishment of death, and they would be replaced with new tenants.

- Upon hearing this parable, only Luke indicates the religious leaders responded by saying, "God forbid" (Luke 20:16).

- Afterward, all three accounts refer to Jesus quoting the Psalms (118:22-23).

- Only Matthew declares the following words by Jesus, "The Kingdom of God will be taken away from you and given to a nation producing fruit of it." Matthew 21:44

- At the end of this parable, there are slight variations such as the religious leaders wanting to arrest Jesus because they perceived the parable was targeting them. However, they refused to do so due to the people's attraction to Jesus' teaching. Even further, only Matthew refers to him as a prophet.

5. What applications can we make for our lives?

I am a keen observer of people and try to learn from their behavior. It is amazing to see how people go about claiming things without having rightful entitlement. For example, the British took the land from the Native Americans. The USA, Europe, Arabs, and Asians are taking raw materials from Africa, so who is holding them accountable? God owns the land and provided the minerals and raw materials, wherein there is more than enough to go around. Instead, greed, and gluttony has caused a serious problem. Let me share a few questions for you to consider.

- Why did the tenants beat, stone, and kill the servants?

- Why would the tenants kill the owner's son?

- What will ultimately happen to those who mistreat God's servants and sons?

- What really happens to those who receive the message of the Kingdom?

6. Can you tell the story in your own words?

This parable serves as a spiritual indictment against both the religious leaders in Israel and Judah. Furthermore, it is a clear illustration of rejecting the prophets who came before Christ and ultimately rejected the Messiah. God has made available an abundance of blessings for all of us to share, but covetousness has overshadowed the act of sharing. The wicked vinedresser did not own the vineyard, but when the harvest came he wanted to keep it all to himself. Not only was the vineyard planted (Church), but God has put in place a safety mechanism, such as the tower to keep away the predators (Satan). However, it is disheartening to see God being disrespected by the same people he entrusted. This parable is a clear reminder persecution will occur, but the consequences will be severe for evil in the end. The righteous are servants and sons. On the one hand, a faithful servant works diligently on behalf of another and does not expect an inheritance. On the other hand, a son also works on the estate, but he is entitled to receive an inheritance, ultimately. The wicked tenants thought by killing the son: the result would enable them to seize the estate. Likewise, religious and civic leaders felt killing Jesus would eradicate this new teaching and sustain their religious institution. Instead, the death of Jesus brought down the wrath of God, while ushering in the Kingdom of God. In closing, we must always keep our ears and hearts open to the messengers from the Kingdom and collectively share in the fruit emanating from the Great Harvest.

17. The Wedding Feast
(Matthew 22:2-14)

Comments

We will treat this as a single parable. However, there is a similar account in Luke 14:16-24. In that instance, it is called a banquet instead of a wedding.

The parable continues a similar pattern of the previous one in this chapter. It is clear Jesus utilized this story to serve as a spiritual indictment against the leaders in Israel.

From antiquity, weddings have served as a joyful occasion because it served as an official and legal platform to expand the family and community. In this instance, an invitation was extended to a particular with the courier being beaten and killed instead of accepted. Subsequently, we will observe judgment carried out on several fronts, while the wedding feast continued.

1. What are the circumstances surrounding the origin of this parable?

In the previous parable we were able to place Jesus at the temple in Jerusalem (Matthew 21:23) shedding some light on the spiritual state of Israel prior to the crucifixion.

2. Who is the parable addressed to?

While at the temple, He is teaching before the chief priest and elders and expounding upon the Kingdom of God. Therefore, Jesus is speaking specifically to religious leaders.

3. What is the subject drawn from?

The parable is drawn from a common experience. Listed are a few observations:

- The New Testament term *Gamos* refers to marriage or wedding feast, whereby two are joined, together. Generally speaking, in Hebraic customs, the marriage supper took place in the husband's house and was a great social event in family life.

- A king represents nobility and authority. Therefore, one expects a favorable response when he sends an invitation.

- The servants delivered the invitations (verbally) to certain invited guests to attend the wedding feast.

- A certain invited guest refused the invitation and set forth a few excuses.

- Another delegation was sent and highlighted the great sacrifice or preparation for this communal gathering.

- Once again, they ignored the invitation and displayed the following responses: One returned to his farm; another returned to his business; and others seized, tortured, and killed the servant.

- Upon hearing the news, the king got very angry and sent a military entourage to destroy them and their community.

- Afterward, the king reiterates the wedding must go on as scheduled, despite this unfortunate situation.

- The invitation list is expanded by inviting persons without clout or social status. The term *thoroughfare* or *highway* stems from the New Testament word *Hodos* and basically means a road, way, or path frequently traveled.

- The servants invite and gather both likeable and unlikeable individuals to attend the wedding.

- Once the crowd gathered, the king entered and immediately observed a guest with inappropriate attire.

- The man is questioned about his attire; why was he dressed inappropriately?

- The man was speechless.

- The improperly dressed man is bound, beaten, and removed from the wedding.

- The parable ends by reminding us there is a calling (summons), but there is also an election (chosen)

4. Variations in the Gospels.

As mentioned earlier this parable is found only in Matthew.

5. What applications can we make for our lives?

Thanksgiving, Christmas, Kwanzaa, weddings, family reunion etc. are great example where family and friends come together in fellowship. Generally speaking, there are official and unofficial dress codes. Putting the attire issue aside, how would you feel if a dear friend or family member snubbed your invitation after all the sacrifice and energy you put into the event? Sharing or fellowshipping is essential for the faith community although from time to time personally you may not want to attend.

6. Can you tell the story in your own words?

The king represents the ultimate authority, God. He has prepared a great wedding feast, wherein the redeemed of the Lord can attend (Revelation chapter 19). In the Old Testament, Yahweh symbolically married Israel just like Christ marries the Church.

Everyday, I observe people rejecting and abusing God's messengers, but rest assured these acts will not go unpunished. Divine judgment came against those who abused the messengers as well as those who were improperly dressed at the wedding feast. Please do not dwell on the treatment of the improperly dressed man, but rather on the appropriate wedding garment (righteousness).

Each of us must allow our heart and soul to be redeemed from a life of unrighteousness and show reverence to Jesus Christ as Lord and Savior. The Great Invitation is yet extended and very soon the marriage will take place. What will be your response to the invitation, and how will you be dressed? No one can stop the invitation from going out, and neither can any of you stop the judgment due to inappropriate behavior. Thank God for the Great Invitation and more so for the union with Christ.

18. The Fig Tree
(Matthew 24:32-35; Mark 13:28-32 & Luke 21:29-33)

Comments

Please keep in mind parables are uniquely placed in the New Testament as a means of teaching about the Kingdom of God. The term *parable* derives from the Greek word *Parabole*. Generally speaking, it means to place alongside, to throw, parallel, or make comparison. We appreciate these colorful stories, but should never lose sight of the underlying truth expressed in each one.

This parable serves as a symbol or reminder of Israel's state of being. It is relatively short, but precise. We will take note of Jesus in Jerusalem entering the final stages of His ministry. It is presented as a wake-up call to become cognizant of the times and seasons we are living in. It also serves as one of seven occasions where we have three accounts of the same story. Even further, it is the last parable where we observe three accounts of the same.

1. What are the circumstances surrounding the origin of this parable?

- Both Matthew and Mark record Jesus sitting on the Mount of Olives (Matthew 24:3 & Mark 13:3) disclosing revelations about the last days.

- Luke placed Jesus at the Temple (21:5) in Jerusalem. At any rate, Luke concurs with the other gospel writers by describing the grueling realities permeating around divine judgment in and around Jerusalem.

- Jesus remarks about the destruction of the temple and other disasters seemed unbelievable at the time.

2. Who is the parable addressed to?

- Matthew indicates the disciples privately came to Jesus while He was in devotion at the Mount of Olives (24:3)

- Mark gives a similar report; however, he specified four disciples: Peter, James, John, and Andrew (13:3).

- Luke does not identify the person(s) but rather indicates someone in and around the temple addressed Him as Teacher (21:7).

3. What is the subject drawn from?

- Remember parables are drawn from common experiences or scenes of nature.

- Jesus utilized a fig tree not producing in her season, thus we call it a scene from nature.

- The Old Testament term *Peri* refers to fruit, reward, result, offspring, and product.

- The New Testament term *Sukon* denotes fig, and *Suke/Sukea* refers to a fig tree.

- In Palestine, a fig tree with leaves indicates young fruit, or it will be barren for the year. They usually ripen in May or June. In some cases, fig trees bear fruit early under the leaves and the later fruit above the leaves.

4. Variations in the Gospels.

- Both Matthew and Mark give a verbatim account in the opening verses.

- The term *summer* in our text derives from the Greek word *Theros*. This season is easily identified due to the prolonged heat. In addition, this is the season to manifest and show signs of reproduction just like the fig tree.

- According to the Revised Standard Version, Luke is the only one who used the term *parable*. In addition, Luke mentioned the fig tree and other trees.

- Luke mentions the relationship with the fig tree and summer in the second verse.

- Matthew and Mark used the term gate metaphorically as a reminder Christ is associated with the season (summer) and the delightful fruit (produce).

- Luke does not use the term gate in the parable. Instead, he introduces the phrase *Kingdom of God*. Remember, the KOG is the sphere of God's reign, territorially and governmentally speaking.

- Matthew, Mark, and Luke basically say the same thing by referring to the generation at hand. The Old Testament term *Dor* refers to a period during which people live and hold things in common. The New Testament term *Genea/Genesis* has to do with origin, lineage, birth, and offspring.

- In essence, this parable is pronouncing divine judgment on the leadership and people living in and around Jerusalem.

- The phrase *heaven and earth* serves as contrasting views of life, such as the temporal and eternal. For the most part, the Church has presented a shallow interpretation regarding the truth and realities of heaven and earth.

- The Old Testament term for heaven is *Samayim.* The term includes the realm of the sky (Deuteronomy 4:17); area farther removed from the earth (Job 38:29); the realm where the sun, moon, and stars are located (Genesis 1:14 & Psalms 104:2); the entire creation (Genesis 1:1) and the dwelling place of God (Psalms 2:4 & Deuteronomy 10:14)

- The New Testament term *Ouranos & Ouranios* gives us a broad view of the meaning of heaven. It refers to the sky (Revelation 6:14); eternal dwelling place of God (Matthew 5:16); eternal dwelling place of the saints (2 Corinthians 5:1); place where Christ sits in divine authority (Ephesians 1:20) and above the earth (Philippians 2:10).

- The earth is clearly the manifestation of God's glory (Psalms 24:1). The heavens and earth appears to be in transition. However, the Word of God represents the mind, will, intent and spiritual or sacred concerns. Therefore, the Word always remains creative, redeeming and revealing.

5. What applications can we make for our lives?

The budding of the fig tree in summer signifies the Coming of Christ. It is an indication for us to be mindful the judgment or decision-making is at hand. Scripturally, the fig tree was noted as a persistent food in Israel, but it also served as a token of peace and spiritual favor. God has given us an opportunity (Grace) to produce in the summer of your life.

The summer represents a heightened awareness regarding the mission of the Church. You cannot afford to pretend or behave like the hypocrite and hide behind the leaves of religion, rituals, a form of godliness, and fail to produce fruit of righteousness in this Dispensation of Grace. Remember, good seed planted in good soil is destined to produce good fruit.

6. Can you tell the story in your own words?

Spiritually, each of you must recognize and accept the truth. Jesus used the fig tree because it is delicious, nutritious, and well recognized in the area. The proof of the pudding is in the eating, and you definitely know it is summer by looking at the behavior of the fig tree. The budding of the tree reminds us summer is coming and so will the return of Christ occur for all to see. However, there will be no opportunity to get ready upon His return. His coming will bring judgment on the nations and individuals due to hypocrisy and unrighteousness.

The fig tree differs from most fruit trees in that its fruit is green, inconspicuous, and concealed among leaves until near the time of ripening. Likewise, the saints are kept and shielded from the world through the Holy Spirit until the return of Christ. Pay close attention to the seasons and be seen budding in the summer, so that at His return you will be able to rejoice.

19. The Wise and Foolish Virgins
(Matthew 25:1-13)

Comments

Parables are enlightening and colorful stories pertaining to the Kingdom of God. Bottom line, you should not be carried away with the details of the story but open the heart and ears to the underlying truth being conveyed.

This parable is next to the last found in Matthew. It gives us a glimpse into the marriage customs in Israel during the first century A.D. You will observe similarities and differences between the comparisons of this marriage custom and the USA.

Nonetheless, this marriage serves as a wake-up call for religious leaders and the Church at large. We must allow the Holy Spirit (oil) to always shine and govern our behavior, so we will be ready to receive the Bridegroom (Christ) upon His return. In order to drive the message home to the listeners, Jesus talks about five wise and five foolish virgins waiting for the opportunity to attend the wedding.

The Bridegroom is very late arriving for some unknown reason. The oil runs out in the five foolish virgins' lamps as a result of this delay, and precisely at this juncture, we will see a divine act of judgment being pointed out and only half of the virgins were able to accompany the Bridegroom.'

1. What are the circumstances surrounding the origin of this parable?

The previous parable of the Fig Tree indicated Jesus was sitting on the Mount of Olives (24:3), sharing a revelation or prophecy about the devastation of Jerusalem.

2. Who is the parable addressed to?

It appears the disciples approached Jesus and wanted some clarity about the upcoming catastrophic events that will soon take place.

3. What is the subject drawn from?

- If we consider the terms *lamps, bridegroom,* and *wedding*, it is drawn from common experiences.

- From the perspective of the oil, it is drawn from a scene in nature.

4. Variations in the Gospels.

- The parable is found only in Matthew, but the subject marriage is universal and discussed throughout the Bible.

- Some church traditions refer to these virgins as bridesmaids. However, this is not the position I take because bridesmaids would not be waiting for a husband per se.

- Marriage (*gamos*) serves as a sacred covenant between a male and female, and it ought not to be taken, lightly.

- Generally speaking, the young virgins or maidens would gather at a compound with the expectation of being selected as a potential bride. They would wait patiently for the arrival of the bridegroom.

- Customarily, they would wait from dusk until midnight or later.

- The New Testament term *Numphios* denotes bridegroom, or a male who is ready to get married.

- The Old Testament term *Almah* refers to virgins. Virgins refer to all females who are eligible for marriage, but they are not wives, queens nor concubines; a maiden or woman who has not borne a child.

- The New Testament term *Lampas* refers to a small vessel used for the purpose of containing oil. Metaphorically, we are referred to as lamps.

- Five women were wise (*Hakam*) prudent or practical. Five were foolish (*Iwwelet*), stupid, or acted irresponsibly.

- The term *oil* in the New Testament stems from the word *Elaion* and serves as the fuel or source for light contained in a lamp.

- Only the wise carried an extra supply of oil in their vessels or flasks.

- The delay of the bridegroom coming resulted in sleep and exposing the lack of preparation on the part of half the women.

- Midnight denotes a dark period that is between dusk and dawn. It is also a time for divine testing.

- The announcement was made in the compound the bridegroom has come, and it was customary for the virgins to follow him with their glowing lights to his home and share in the wedding feast.

- Traditionally, only one of the women would be selected and married. However, it also served as an opportunity for other men to see potential brides.

- The wise virgins (5) responded in a favorable manner and left with the bridegroom. Alternatively, the foolish (5) responded unfavorably by asking the wise to share some of their oil with them.

- Even further, the foolish virgins left the compound and went in to the community seeking oil, but due to the hour of the night they were unsuccessful.

- Eventually, the foolish virgins went to the wedding feast in the dark due to having no oil in the lamps and knocked on the door. However, they were denied entrance into the wedding feast.

5. What applications can we make for our lives?

As a child, I would often hear my father, and other ministers in the Church of God in Christ expound on this text. The parable clearly reminds us there is a thin line between paying and not paying attention to spiritual concerns. Patience is a virtue, but it is only effective when you allow the Holy Spirit (oil) to flow and operate within our container (you). Each of you must do his or her best and make sure you are prepared and qualified to attend the marriage feast.

6. Can you tell the story in your own words?

The *Church* is compared to a *Bride* that is patiently waiting for the *Bridegroom.* Virgins are depicted as pure and righteous women who are expected to reproduce and bring forth righteous fruit in the Kingdom of God. The Lord has purposefully delayed His return, but it ought not to cause you to act irresponsibly. The invitation to the wedding was extended to the ten virgins, but only half ended up going in. Be watchful and prayerful because the Lord will return at a time least expected and escort us to the *Great Marriage Feast* around the *Throne of God.*

20. The Talents
(Matthew 25:14-30)

Comments

We have reached the final parable in Matthew. Altogether, there are 20 parables recorded in Matthew. Only Luke has more parables (27) recorded than Matthew.

As mentioned before, parables are colorful and insightful stories drawn from nature or insightful realities, also known as common experience. Jesus skillfully utilized these stories to help unlock the mysteries pertaining to the Kingdom of God. Therefore, it is important for you to focus on the truth being conveyed rather than details in the parables.

In this parable, we will observe the owner of an estate distributing *talents* to several tenants or servants. Meanwhile, the men were expected to manage and yield an increase from the talents entrusted to them as he departs for an extended period of time. However, we will observe a favorable report from two of them and an unfavorable report from one.

1. What are the circumstances surrounding the origin of this parable?

It appears Jesus is teaching and prophesying from the Mount of Olives (Mt. 24:3) regarding the inevitable destruction against Jerusalem and Judah.

2. Who is the parable addressed to?

Jesus is responding to questions raised by the disciples as they gathered around Him.

3. What is the subject drawn from?

Jesus used a common experience (talents) to expose the strengths and weaknesses of men given an assignment.

- The New Testament term *Talan ton* refers to a balance, sum of money, weight in gold or silver, or a gift or an assignment.

- The term *Property* in scripture derives from the Hebrew word *Ahuzzah.* It is a legal term usually used for land.

4. Variations in the gospels.

- The parable is found only in Matthew.

- The owner of the estate made plans to travel, and prior to departing, he summoned three servants to oversee his properties. Take note, he did not tell them what to do with the talents, but it seemed they already knew what was expected of them.

- He distributed the talents, accordingly: One servant received 5 talents; one servant received 2 talents and one servant received 1 talent.

- It has been suggested each talent had an estimated value of $1,000.00. If so, we are talking about a sizeable amount of value for that era.

- Each man was given (a talent) according to his ability or character based upon the owner's knowledge of the same.

- The servant with the most talents (5) immediately went to work and maximized the yield of these talents by doubling the talents and gained five more.

- The servant with two talents displayed the same spirit by doubling the talents and gained two more.

- However, the servant with one talent played it cautiously safe and buried the talent until the owner returned.

- After a considerable period of time, the owner returned and summoned the servants to give an account of the talents left with them.

- He was pleased with the reports submitted by the men having five and two talents, and simply said, "*Well done, good and faithful servants.*"

- However, the man with the least amount of reported talents (1) displeased the owner because of an inert/lazy behavior.

- The owner takes the one talent from him and gives it to the one who had the five talents. In addition, he banished the man with the single talent from fellowshipping in the kingdom.

5. What applications can we make for our lives?

It does not take much effort to make excuses if you are afraid to venture out in life. Being comfortable seems to be a safe and appropriate course of action. The mere fact that an official puts his trust in you with valuable properties should serve notice for you to remain faithful and focused on your assignment at all times. Furthermore, we observed the wisdom of the owner distributing talents without explaining his actions. Sometimes, distribution of life seems unfair. However, you should dedicate yourself in putting forth your best effort instead of putting the blame on anyone (excuse making).

6. Can you tell the story in your own words?

Jesus masterfully expressed the truth by showing the disciples were spiritually mandated to give their best on behalf of the Kingdom of God. Talents or resources may be distributed in manners that we may or may not readily understand, but you must work with what you have on hand. Trying to distribute assignments on an equal basis to everyone is not always a good idea. Each of you must open your ears, hearts, and eyes to what is really going on.

Obviously, the religious leaders played it safe and failed to go beyond their comfort zone. Christ has given the assignments, ascended to heaven, and will return one day to receive the faithful ones. The unfaithful will not be allowed to enter into the kingdom to spend eternity.

Lastly, we observe the man with the worst report getting more attention than the two who had favorable reports. Even further in this life, the unfaithful report gets more attention than the righteous deeds carried out every day.

21. The Growing Seed
(Mark 4:26-29)

Comments

This marks the 21st and next to the last parable in Mark. It is a relatively short but insightful parable, wherein Jesus shares profound thoughts regarding the Kingdom of God.

It should be noted there is a mystery and teachable moment behind the seed that will eventually be revealed. The seed is mandated to be planted, germinate, and grow. There is a similar parable in Matthew 13:24-30. What appears to be a secret ends up being beneficial at harvest time, so it is with the Kingdom of God!

1. What are the circumstances surrounding the origin of this parable?

Earlier in this chapter, we observed Jesus teaching about the kingdom through a series of parables near the Sea of Galilee.

2. Who is the parable addressed to?

It appears Jesus is responding to questions raised by his disciples and others surrounding Him (Mk. 4:10). Please keep in mind parables are primarily addressed to the disciples, multitude, and religious leaders. Nonetheless, it is important for everyone to be attentive.

3. What is the subject drawn from?

This parable is drawn from a scene of nature. In this instance, Jesus refers to seeds being planted. The Hebrew term *Nata* refers to planting or establishing something. The Greek term *Sperma* denotes a seed, off-spring or botanical. The seed is the link to the past and future. However, in order to appreciate her fullest potential, it has to be planted in the soil.

4. Variations in the Gospels.

- This particular parable is found only in Mark.

- Scattering (Greek word *skorpiz*a) seeds refers to dispersing or sowing them over a vast area as opposed to a restricted location.

- There is a unique relationship between the dry seed and fertile ground.

- Reference to sleep and awakening denotes period and time frames in our lives that move along according to divine providence.

- While we are in either posture (asleep or awake), the seed has a mandate to grow, but we cannot see it occurring day or night.

- All we can observe is the blade/grass (*chrotos*) as an initial sign of reproduction. Once it is fully grown, the farmer harvests it, but always keeps enough seeds to repeat the cycle.

5. What application can we make for our lives?

The most valuable organs in the human body are hidden beneath our skin. Religion, rituals and traditions cannot substitute the spiritual mandates of the Kingdom of God. As faithful believers in Christ, there is a hidden nature grounded in holiness, which is always trying to bring out the best in us. You may not physically see love, joy, peace, and longsuffering, but they are there as long as we remain spiritually in the soil of the Kingdom of God.

6. Can you tell the story in your own words?

Jesus shared a powerful and revelatory parable pertaining to growth within the Kingdom of God within a world that can be very hostile. Furthermore, this expansion is beyond our understanding and control. Each of us may recognize and learn from living organism, such as the church. Do your part. However, no one can abort or destroy the mystery and the truth inherent in the seed. The seed of righteousness is always growing secretly in the heart of the believer.

22. The Absent Householder
(Mark 13-33-37)

Comments

Keep in mind, parables are insightful stories pertaining to the Kingdom of God and not mere human interest stories. This is the twenty-second parable that serves as the last one in the Gospel according to Mark. For the most part, this parable and the ones to follow are relatively short (with a few exceptions) but are profound.

Sometimes, parables are introduced without the typical words or phrase *Kingdom of God* or mentioning the term *parable.* In this case, Jesus seized the opportunity to shed light or teach kingdom principles, such as accountability and truthfulness. Too often, the faith community seems to misbehave, especially when the person in authority is absent. I will always cherish the words of my high school principal when he said, "Do right, because it is right to do right." Let us study this parable, while also factoring in a sense of judgment (apocalypse).

1. What are the circumstances surrounding the origin of this parable?

In order to fully appreciate this parable, let us visualize the Mount of Olives (Mark 13:3) in the backdrop and Jesus disclosing pertinent information about spiritual judgment earmarked for Jerusalem and Judah (covenant community).

2. Who is the parable addressed to?

It appears Jesus is speaking specifically to some of the disciples, namely Peter, James, John, and Andrew (13:3). However, parables addressed to the disciples may also have spiritual and ethical implications for the multitude and religious leaders.

3. What is the subject drawn from?

- Parables are generally drawn from a common experience or scenes of nature.

- The parable of the *householder* is drawn from a common experience.

- The phrase *take heed* denotes paying attention.

- The term *householder* is found in the New Testament and refers to one who occupies or owns a house or estate. They are the head of the family estate.

4. Variations in the Gospels.

- This parable is found only in Mark.

- Jesus begins this parable by reminding all of us to be watchful especially as it relates to his or her assignment. Furthermore, it remains a secret when the householder will return.

- The phrase *Son of Man,* biblically speaking, refers to Jesus: the anointed servant for humanity on behalf of the Kingdom of God. In this instance, the

Son of Man is illustrated in the householder. It was not unusual for the householder to take extended trips and leave the affairs in the hands of overseers, servants, porters, or gatekeepers until he returned.

- Everyone was instructed regarding his or her assignments and fully aware the householder would return. Jesus makes reference to the distinct watches or time frame in the course of a day.

- He may return in the evening (1st watch of the night).

- He may return at midnight (between night and day)

- He may return at the cockcrowing (prior to daybreak).

- He may return in the morning (after the sun appears).

- The return will be sudden and unannounced because it serves as an act of judgment.

- Reference to sleep serves as an indication the householder acted irresponsibly and did not pay attention during a critical period.

- Jesus concludes this parable by admonishing the disciples as well as others to be watchful.

5. What applications can we make for our lives?

For some reason, people tend to get relaxed or allow his or her self be placed in compromising positions, especially when there is much latitude. For example, a term paper is announced by the teacher at the beginning of the semester that it is due at the end; a substitute teacher occasionally creates an environment for misbehavior, and parents, absent from the house for an extended period of time with unsupervised children, are just a few illustrations of people failing to do their best. Satan delights in laziness, excuse-making, irresponsibility, and procrastination.

6. Can you tell the story in your own words?

This story is an eye-opener because it challenges each of us to be responsible at all times. Giving assignments and going on an extended journey and returning at an unspecified time seems to resonate both a *prophetic* challenge as well as an *apocalyptic* message for the covenant community.

Jesus established the Church via the Kingdom of God, and He has adequately equipped her with Spiritual Gifts until His glorious return. We must not allow the enticement or entrapment of Satan to cause you to act irresponsibly because it appears no one is watching. Our calling is holy, and our mandate is grounded in holiness, faith, and love. Christ will return and only those who are genuinely engaged in Kingdom Ministry will be prepared to meet and return with Him. Are you a faithful and watchful witness?

23. The Creditor and Two Brothers
(Luke 7:41-43)

Comments

This marks the twenty-third parable shared by Jesus. Parables are remarkable and insightful illustrations placed alongside lessons pertaining to the Kingdom of God. The Gospel According to Luke, shares more parables than the other Synoptic Gospels (Mark and Matthew). Altogether, there are twenty-seven parables in Luke. This parable and the remaining seventeen will be found only in Luke.

There are some schools of thought that may not recognize this illustration as a parable, but we will. For example, you do not observe some of the typical words or phrases associated with parables, such as *Kingdom of Heaven/God* or *He taught them in parables saying...* Nonetheless, in this parable we will observe Jesus sharing a profound lesson on the virtue of *forgiveness* in both the physical and spiritual dimensions of life.

1. What are the circumstances surrounding the origin of this parable?

It appears from earlier verses in this chapter, Jesus is in the Province of Galilee or specifically the town of Nain (7:11), which was southeast of Nazareth. Apparently, Jesus was invited to dine at the home of a Pharisee (7:36). Meanwhile, a woman of the city (harlot), presumed to be Mary Magdalene, was not invited before she came into the house. She was keenly aware who Jesus was and therefore, knelt down, wept and wiped his feet with her tears, hair and oil. Of course this demonstration of humility, compassion, love and worship caused a great stir amongst the religious leaders and crowd.

2. Who is the parable addressed to?

On the one hand, it is addressed to the religious leader, a Pharisee who invited Jesus to his home, simply because he was puzzled or stunned about Jesus' refusal to condemn the woman. Instead of condemning her, Jesus allowed her to carry on. Alternatively, Jesus singles Peter out regarding this moment of truth. Thus, the parable is addressed to the religious leaders and the disciples.

3. What is the subject drawn from?

- The parable is drawn from a common experience.

- The term *Creditor* stems from the New Testament Greek word, *Danistes.* The term refers to a money lender or a person with means assisting someone in need.

- The term *Debtor* stems from the New Testament word, *Opheiletes.* The term has to do with a person who owes something to another, usually in regards to money.

4. Variations in the Gospels.

- This parable is found only in Luke, however, there are similar parables pertaining to the relationship between the debt and debtor.

- Debts are universal because there will always be someone faced with a financial challenge and the need for assistance in settling the account.

- The details are not given in this parable surrounding the origin of the two debts.

- Who serves as the money-lender and who is the creditor?

- The following is acknowledged: One man owed five hundred denarii ($100.00) based upon denarii equals twenty cents or twenty month wages. The other man owed fifty denarii ($10.00) or two month wages.

- It is obvious in both instances, the men could not pay the debt and upon facing the debtors, neither were required thereafter. Therefore, the wisdom and mercy of the creditor simply forgave the debts.

- Subsequently, Jesus asked Simon which one loved the creditor more. Simon answered by saying the one who was forgiven the greater debt.

- Jesus re-affirms Simon's answer, by saying, "You have judged rightly."

5. What applications can we make for our lives?

It does not take much to be caught up in a world of debt. Usually, when debts occur, there is a tremendous amount of pressure and tension. There is a spiritual, ethical, and legal dimension to handling debt. If you owe someone, then according to the terms and agreements entered into, you are obligated to repay. However, there are times and circumstances when you must turn inwardly and allow the mercies of God speak to your heart regarding this legal matter. A debt is an open-ended contract (verbal or non-verbal) that needs to be settled, sooner or later.

6. Can you tell the story in your own words?

As usual, Jesus masterfully demonstrates poise and wisdom in this parable. He entered the home of a religious leader (Pharisee) known to be a harsh critic. Houses during this era seemed to have been somewhat open to public intrusion of this nature. The Pharisees, by and large, were considered righteous according to the Law, whereas the woman in our story is presumed to be a sinner. Even further, I believe the disciples were in limbo as to what was really going on. Spiritually speaking, Jesus was there to alleviate the debt of the Pharisee, as reflected in the 50 denarii, but they were too proud or self-righteous to see what was really going on with this woman. However, the woman displayed remorse, worshipped Jesus, and gave of her possession. We too must recognize the small and greater debts owed to God, while receiving His forgiveness.

The parable also illustrates the comparative nature of people and degrees of indebtedness. Nonetheless, God's grace and mercies are always available to forgive and present a new lease on life. If you truly appreciate all the wonderful things Christ has done on your behalf, there is no need to refuse forgiving others. Please do not allow your attitude, pride, things, status or any circumstance get in the way of forgiveness.

24. The Good Samaritan
(Luke 10:29-37)

Comments

This undoubtedly is one of the biblical classics and most widely utilized both within and outside of the church family. Learning to share is at the core of fulfilling the mission of the church and experience a wholesome life. Sometimes, the opportunity to assist others in need may create altered plans and a little inconvenience. However, whenever you ignore a dire need, it gets God's attention and may eventually get out of hand.

This parable is found only in Luke. It should be noted, Luke introduces Jesus as the Universal Savior, simply because, He includes those who are not necessarily accepted or recognized in religious or traditional circles.

Jesus utilizes several individuals in this parable to illustrate what it takes to be a true representative of the Kingdom of God. It is great to have faith, but she must be complimented with work or ministry. Take a look at what Jesus points out:

- The *Hebrew Man*, a victim robbed, wounded, and left on the side of the road.

- The *Hebrew Priest,* represented the religious circle, but failed to help the man in need.

- The *Hebrew Levite,* represented someone skillful in religious circle, also failed to help.

- The *Samaritan* represented the Universal Church although culturally speaking estranged from Israel (covenant community) stopped and helped the man.

- Jesus gives us a more-in-depth answer to the question, who is your neighbor?

1. What are the circumstances surrounding the origin of this parable?

It appears Jesus is commissioning other disciples and teaching about the Kingdom of God. Meanwhile, a lawyer stood up to test/challenge Jesus on the perquisite for obtaining eternal life? (10:25)

2. Who is the parable addressed to?

On the surface, it is addressed to the lawyer. However, we should always keep in mind parables are addressed to the disciples, multitude, and religious leaders.

3. What is the subject drawn from?

The parable is drawn from a common experience as suggested in the topic *Good Samaritan.* The man responds to a need versus a scene from nature.

4. Variations in the Gospels.

There are no comparisons with the other gospel because only Luke records this story. Nonetheless, here are a few observations:

- The New Testament term *Nomikos* refers to a Hebrew who was skilled in Mosaic Law.

- Lawyers are noted for interrogating; therefore, he wanted to know who my neighbor is. The N.T. term *Geiton* denotes one living in the same land or shares something in common.

- Jesus gives a profound illustration pertaining to the way we should view our neighbors.

- The Jericho Road was notorious for thieves and robbers.

- The city of Jericho was situated northeast of Jerusalem along a mountainous path.

- Jesus tells a story about a man who was traveling this road, and became victimized by robbers. Afterward, they beat him and left him to die.

- Eventually, a priest (Hb. term *Kohen* and Gk. Term *Hiereus*) came along and saw the beaten man, *he* but refused to get involved. More than likely, he was on his way to perform religious duties. Remember, the priest held the highest religious leadership in Israel.

- Later that same day, a Levite passed by and beheld the same destitute man on the side of the road. Instead of helping him, he too ignored the man and continued on his journey. The Levite served as a lay-associate of the priest in the temple.

- Finally, a Samaritan, who was considered a foreigner, yet had Hebraic Ancestry, observed a man in dire need, pushed aside excuses and prejudices, and simply stopped to display compassion.

- He applied oil (anointing) and wine (healing) to the wounded man in addition to taking him to a more secured place, an Inn, whereby he might recover.

- He gave the innkeeper two denarii (40 cents) to help take care of the injured man.

- The Samaritan had to continue his journey, but assured the innkeeper he would return and cover any additional cost incurred by this guest.

- Jesus concludes this parable by asking the lawyer, which of the three displayed a neighborly spirit?

- The lawyer chose the Samaritan as the one who showed mercy, and Jesus confirmed his answer.

- Jesus concludes by admonishing him to take this same spirit and apply it in all situations.

5. What applications can we make for our lives?

The world we live in is full of circumstances that pop up and need immediate attention, but far too often, men and women opt to ignore them. It is one thing to say you love the world, while stepping over the person who is next door or in your path.

In far too many instances, *church-folks* have become too comfortable with the grueling realities along their religious path. For example, there is truth in this quote, "Our children are growing up like weeds on a vacant lot." The neglect of the children and elders are prime examples of need going unattended. There are other realities often ignored: Drugs, alcohol, violence, education, health, economic, government, and family etc.

6. Can you tell the story in your own words?

Once again, Jesus masterfully indicted the religious community for failing to represent the Kingdom of God in a compassionate and practical manner. There are too many people who are *so heavenly minded until they are no earthly good.* Religion is designed to promote worship, ethics, and service.

Striking a balance in a wayward world is a great challenge for people moving along through life. Interestingly, God seems to allow various situations to occur that often are ugly and distasteful, whereby you might have the opportunity (grace) to do something about it.

The truth is all of us have a degree of prejudice and tend to ignore realities that need attention. However, no one should allow any victim to go unattended even if you are on your way somewhere. Good works alone cannot merit salvation, but good works are the result of spiritual awareness. The church cannot afford to become so occupied about his or her status and where they are going, while stepping over the persons suffering along the way. The Good Samaritan represents the man or woman whom you least expect to help. Trouble does not discriminate. The world is our neighbor, and Jesus is watching the way you handle these situations as you travel through life.

25. The Friend in Need
(Luke 11:5-13)

Comments

This is the twenty-fifth parable shared by Jesus. He faithfully and methodically used parables as a means of unlocking the mysteries embedded in the Kingdom of God. In this parable, Jesus seems to be expanding upon the earlier parable of the Good Samaritan. We are about to explore the righteous and appropriate response of a friend addressing a need at an inopportune time. Furthermore, we notice Jesus emphasizing the benefits of being persistent.

1. What are the circumstances surrounding the origin of this parable?

In the latter part of the previous chapter, it appears Jesus was in Bethany at the home of a friend (Lazarus) and his sisters (Mary and Martha). This chapter opens with Jesus praying in a familiar place, presumed to be the *Mount of Olives.* Therefore, this parable surfaces because Jesus wants to emphasize the value and ultimate benefits of prayer.

2. Who is the parable address to?

One of the disciples requested Jesus to teach them how to pray, just as John the Baptist taught his disciples (11:1). Therefore, the parable is addressed to the disciples, but has resounding benefits for everyone.

3. What is the subject drawn from?

This parable is drawn from a common experience, because it discloses a need, and the response of a friend.

- The New Testament Greek term *Chrezo* denotes a need. Biblically speaking, a need is a necessity or experiencing the lack of something that is essential.

- The Old Testament Hebrew word *Rea* refers to a friend. A friend is a companion or someone you have a reciprocal relation with.

4. Variations in the Gospels.

- This parable is found only in Luke. However, there are some parallels with the *Parable of the Unjust Judge* (Luke 18:1-5).

- Jesus begins by mentioning a friend who was faced with a challenge at midnight due to not having bread on hand to feed a guest who just arrived.

- Being hospitable to a guest upon arrival was very important. It appears the guest came unannounced or later than expected.

- The friend or host in the house has nothing prepared to offer this weary traveler. Therefore, he leaves home and goes to a friend nearby seeking bread.

- He knocks on the door at midnight and briefly explained what is going on. Meanwhile, the friend, his wife, and children are sleeping.

- Initially, the friend inside insisted he leave, before he disturbed others in the house.

- Meanwhile, the friend standing outside persists, and the text introduced the term *importunity.* The Greek term *Anaidia* has to do with shameless persistence can result in a favorable response.

- The friend inside eventually got up and supplied the friend outside with the bread.

- Verse 9 gives a brief explanation regarding the meaning of the parable, by telling us there are benefits for those who put forth a genuine and faithful effort, such as asks, seeks, and knocks. The plural use of these terms reflects persistency and determination.

- Jesus went a little further talking about friendship and prayer by using the analogy of a son asking his father for a fish. Do you expect the father to give him a serpent instead?

- In the earthly dimension of life, we know how to be cordial and civil toward each other. Then, how much more will our *Heavenly Father* grant us the gift of the Holy Spirit, as a means to govern our life?

5. What applications can we make for our lives?

Foundationally speaking, each of you should embrace a prayerful life.   In short, the term *prayer* stems from the Old Testament Hebrew term *Palal* referring to intervening, petitioning, requesting, whereby an official makes a judgment/ruling in an important matter.

There will always be needs and this includes inconvenient moments. When a need arises, it is not the time to make excuses. Each of you should know the difference between a need and someone trying to exploit you. A true friend, also a believer in Christ, will recognize the need and help, while the person in need will not give up until he or she sees the manifestation of what he or she is looking for.

6. Can you tell the story in your own words?

Jesus illustrated in this parable, practical aspects of the Kingdom of God. As a child, I vividly recall my parents getting up late at night to receive a visiting evangelist in our home who did not have a place to stay. In addition, my mother would always prepare a meal and made the guest feel welcome. Even further, the siblings would have to give up his or her room quite often. God is always creating or allowing scenarios of need to surface in order for you to address them.

Let me recap this parable. A friend arrives at the home of a friend late one night, but there was no food on hand. Nonetheless, the friend goes to another friend's house and asks for bread. Initially, the friend inside does not want to get up and politely asks him to leave.

Persistence and sincerity paid off in this story because the need is met. Sometimes, needs have to be met through channels of embarrassment. God is observing your behavior and efforts when needs often arise. I like to end this lesson with inspiring words from someone else.

You are the person who has to decide

Whether you'll do it, or toss it aside.

You are the person who makes up your mind

Whether you'll lead or linger behind.

Whether you'll try for a goal that is far

Or be contented to stay where you are

Take or leave it, there's something to do

Just think it over –

It's all up to you (Anonymous)

The blessings lie beyond the need (bread) and the prayer (asking) you are offering to the Lord is waiting on you.

26. The Rich Fool
(Luke 12:16-21)

Comments

I am amazed at the way people perceive what is most important in life. This parable is very straightforward and simplistic as it reminds us life is full of contrasts or laws of opposites.

We will observe just how generous and gracious God is toward His creation. However, we will also observe just how selfish and greedy people can be in making choices or responding to divine favor. Ultimately, the choice is up to you to make whether wise or foolish. In order to grasp a more comprehensive perspective of this parable, you may want to begin with verse thirteen.

1. What are the circumstances surrounding the origin of this parable?

In the earlier verses, there seem to be a dispute between two brothers pertaining to the distribution of an estate or inheritance. Therefore, Jesus wants to emphasize a few characteristics of the Kingdom of God i.e. humility and fairness versus pride and greed.

2. Who is the parable address to?

According to the text (Luke 12:13), someone from the crowd asked a question directed toward Jesus. Let us assume it is the younger brother seeking clarity about his entitlement being disbursed by the older brother (Deuteronomy 21:17). Therefore, this parable is addressed to the multitude, but it has relevance for the religious leaders and disciples who were standing by.

3. What is the subject drawn from?

- This parable is drawn from a common experience.

- The Old Testament term *Ewil* denotes a fool. A fool lacks wisdom and they are unethical. The New Testament gives us a variety of terms for fools, and in essence, they refer to a person who is void of reasoning, lack of self-control, or behave without discernment.

- The Old Testament term for land is *Adamah.* You can readily see the root word Adam. The land refers to the ground, earth, soil, and property. The New Testament term *Ge* and a host of other terms refer to land. Basically, it entails territory, ground, field, possession, and earth etc.

- The land represents the physical manifestation of God's glory, wherein provisions for sustenance and livelihood are made.

- *Soul* is a widely discussed term in both the Old and New Testament. In short, the soul is identified as the life-force embodied in the human body, conscious core, divine reasoning, and breath. The soul is a spiritual and eternal entity in contrast to the land or physical aspects of life. The soul must be reverenced because her origin is from the Most High God.

4. Variations in the Gospels.

- This parable is found only in Luke. However, Jesus has been persistent in teaching other parables regarding greed and selfishness.

- Jesus responded to a question centered on the distribution of property associated with a rich farmer.

- God owns the land, but allows man and woman to manage, cultivate, and reap the benefits.

- This farmer had an above average harvest and this was cause for a celebration. Therefore, he considered his options.

- Apparently, his barns/vats/storehouses were filled to capacity.

- He decides to tear down the existing ones and construct new ones that will accommodate larger quantities, but at no time is there a mentioning of considering the poor or needy.

- Verse 19, Jesus indicated the rich farmer failed to consider the mission and destiny of the soul within the human arena.

- The phrase, *Eat, drink, and be merry* is associated with an Epicurean Philosophy which emphasized enjoying the pleasures of life. Putting it another way, they promoted *I got mine and the heck with you.*

- In the midst of this narrow-minded celebration, we see an act of divine judgment being announced against the attitude of the rich young farmer. God calls him a fool and asks him what will happen to all these things you have accumulated? There is no space or place in eternity for carnality or materialism.

- Jesus concludes this parable by admonishing everyone to appreciate and utilize the benefits of this earth, but do not become enslaved to the same.

5. What applications can we make for our lives?

No one in his or her right mind delights in being slighted nor neglected in getting a fair share in life. By and large, the poor want to live more comfortably, but who looks out for them? The rich are seldom satisfied with what they have accumulated. There seems to be a tendency to want more. The civil and criminal courts are backlogged with disputes in the USA. The righteous are aware there is provision for them and will not be denied property, food, and aesthetics. I see far too many people bent all out of shape about the way goods are accumulated and shared. God knows how to manage and when to make the shift in His creation.

I heard this assessment of money from an economist years ago regarding the use of it, "You can do the following things with money. You can spend it, save it, invest it, and give it away." I tend to specialize in the giving aspect.

6. Can you tell the story in your own words?

Jesus masterfully drew a parallel between the physical and spiritual dimensions of life. The earth is one of the four essential elements i.e. earth, air, fire, and water created by God and made available for man's use. The acquisition of property occurs in a variety of ways, but the truth remains in knowing the land originates from God. It is one thing to be fiscally prudent and maximize your wealth in this world, but it is more important to not be driven by greed and selfishness. There is more than enough in this world to go around.

Your soul serves as the link to wisdom and eternity. Therefore, what appears seemingly to be a lighthearted gesture may be a blessing in disguise? Lastly, when you receive a blessing, which is spiritual in nature, you must always factor in sharing or passing this along to others. Blessings are preserved for the righteous, and you may never know when and how they will surface. Therefore, I urge you to remain humble, focused, generous, and steadfast.

27. The Watchful Servants
(Luke 12:35-40)

Comments

This parable could easily be labeled *The Unfaithful Servant* due to the inappropriate and appropriate behavior of the servants. Jesus continues to share insights about the Kingdom of God by highlighting the importance of faithfulness.

In the previous parables or teachings (Matthew 24:43-51, 25:1-13 and Mark 13:33-37), Jesus makes it abundantly clear that the servants/stewards are attendants who have been entrusted with the management of the owner's property in his absence.

In this parable, we will observe the *Master* has gone to a *Marriage Feast,* and no one knows precisely when he will return. However, it is anticipated he will return at an inopportune time. Nonetheless, it was clearly the duty of the servant to open the gates, while availing himself to fellowship with the owner upon his return. On the one hand, we must value the time to rest, while on the other hand, fulfill assigned duties, and remain watchful, and responsible. By all means, do not sleep too hard.

1. What are the circumstances surrounding the origin of this parable?

The parable serves as a continuation of Jesus' teachings about the physical versus the spiritual values in life. Therefore, being sensitive and faithful to spiritual concerns will prove to be beneficial.

2. Who is the parable addressed to?

Earlier in the chapter, Jesus seemed to be speaking specifically to the disciples (12:22) about kingdom principles.

3. What is the subject drawn from?

- The parable is drawn from a common experience versus a scene from nature.

- The New Testament gives us several terms for Masters, such as *Didaskalos* (teacher); *Kurios* (Lord or one with authority); *Rabbei* (Jewish Teacher); and *Epistates* (chief, commander or overseer).

- The New Testament terms for Servant are *Doulos* (bondman) and *Oiketes* (household).

- The phrase *wedding feast* stems from the term *Gamos.* Symbolically, it refers to the union of Christ with the Church. In addition, it refers to a joyful occasion surrounding a marriage and reception.

4. Variations in the Gospels.

- This parable is found only in Luke.

- Jesus is revealing a profound lesson on paying attention and being alert as Servants of God.

- Verse 35 introduces several terms such as, *loins, girded* and *lamp.* In essence, they are used metaphorically to challenge us, whereby we tighten up our behavior and watch what is going on at all times.

- The parable discloses a Master who leaves home and attends a wedding feast, which normally suggests being away for an extended period.

- Eventually, the master returns home and expects the gates to open rapidly regardless of current time of the night.

- Verse 37 indicates the servants who responded quickly will be blessed; receiving gifts or rewards from the Master.

- Instead of the Master being served, He served the servant for being on his post.

- The Master's arrival is not predictable by the servants. For example, he could come in the 2nd night watch (9 PM to Midnight) or the 3rd night watch (Midnight to 3 AM). The bottom line is everyone knows the Master will definitely return, and the faithful servants will be blessed.

- The New Testament term for Householder is *Oikodespotes.* This term denotes a Goodman, Master of the house, or one in charge of the house. Jesus stressed that the person in charge has a responsibility to remain vigilant.

- The analogy also includes the nature of a thief coming unannounced as will be when the Son of Man (Christ) returns.

5. What applications can we make for our lives?

I observe too many people engaged in activities or preoccupied with various, distractive assignments until they forget what is paramount in life. The parable clearly illustrates the way God has entrusted each of us with various responsibilities while He is away. Upon His return, we must be ready to meet Him and offer no excuses.

6. Can you tell the story in your own words?

Jesus is the master of unlocking the mysteries of the Kingdom of God, while rendering an indictment against the religious leaders. We must gird our spiritual loins and safeguard the eternal message. Sleep and fatigue are part of life's equation; however, you cannot make excuses when it comes to being responsible.

Let's suppose you are extremely tired after a long day at work. You have a one-year old child at home you are responsible for. If you ignore the child and fall asleep from exhaustion, you will more than likely face undesirable consequences, later. Instead of Christ returning from the Wedding Feast, He will return to escort the faithful witnesses (bride) to the wedding feast in heaven. Either you are properly adorned in wedding garments (holy), or you will not be ready. Christ's return will not come to get you ready, but you must be ready. The pureness of your heart and reviving of your soul will keep you spiritually alert, so you can hear His knock.

28. The Faithful and Evil Servant
(Luke 12:42-48)

Comments

This marks the third and final parable in this chapter. It is apparent Jesus is sharing further comments surrounding the Kingdom of God in the area of faithfulness and watchfulness.

We are about to explore the behavior of servants or stewards who were entrusted with managing the household while the Master/Owner has gone away. Furthermore, we will observe there was an opportunity to progress in responsibility and status. Instead of being dutiful, we will observe laziness and irresponsibility on behalf of the one in charge. The Master appeared at an unexpected hour, and in so doing the servant in charge of the household had an unfavorable outcome.

1. What are the circumstances surrounding the origin of this parable?

This parable follows immediately after the *Parable of the Watchful Servants.* In this instance, Jesus is expanding His teachings about other aspects or details regarding the kingdom.

2. Who is the parable addressed to?

In verses 41-42, Peter asked a question pertaining to the previous parable, and Jesus responded by introducing another parable. Therefore, the parable is addressed specifically to the disciples. However, the implications are good for the multitude and religious leaders as well.

3. What is the subject drawn from?

- The parable is drawn from a common experience.

- See the previous parable regarding the definitions of servants and masters.

- The New Testament term for household is *Oikeios.* It denotes persons associated with an estate or dwelling place and includes servants and master.

4. Variations in the Gospels.

- This parable is found only in Luke. However, there are similar teachings in Matthew 24:45-51.

- Jesus shared this parable by drawing our attention to a comparison between a faithful and unfaithful servant.

- The master assigned a steward to be over the distribution of food to other servants over a period of time.

- Jesus emphasized there will be benefits (blessings) for the steward who faithfully discharged his or her duties (verse 43).

- The term *truly* stems from the Greek word *Aletheia.* It refers to certainty, verifying, surely, and manifestation. Jesus reminds us that unfaithfulness to a good cause will not go unnoticed in the kingdom.

- However, there is always the potential for a member of the household to behave irresponsibly, simply because they think they can get away with it.

- The story reveals the steward in charge abused his authority and started beating the Master's servants and indulged in eating and drinking excessively (verse 45).

- The Master who gave the assignment will certainly return at a time the steward least expects and administer justice.

- Divine or universal justice may seem cruel or unmerciful, but it serves as a reminder you cannot do wrong and without consequence.

- Verse 48 reveals an interesting perspective. For example, everyone is accountable and, based upon the knowledge received, will be dealt with accordingly (Numbers 15:29-30; Deuteronomy 25:2-3 and Luke 8:18). Justice will always be served, but mercy is always a factor within the divine equation.

- Jesus concludes this parable by reminding each of us there are degrees of responsibilities given in every household. Eventually, everyone must give an account of his or her stewardship before the Master.

5. What applications can we make for our lives?

Within the world we live, there are people displaying various degrees of status or rank. No matter where you live or who you are, there will be those in authority and under authority. Each must do his or her best at all times and not allow excuses to prevail if you desire a favorable outcome in life.

By and large, I see far too many people going through routines like going to church, working, residing in communities, and voting in elections, etc. However, they fail to give his or her best. For example, let's suppose you are currently earning minimum wage on your job. By all means, be thankful and faithful for the income. After all, we know God will reward the faithful and grateful ones.

6. Can you tell the story in your own words?

Jesus masterfully demonstrated the behavior of people throughout all generations. If you give certain individuals a little authority, the flaw in their character will cause them to abuse the same. Furthermore, if you give someone an inch, they will take a mile. Sometimes, we may not like our assignments in life, and that is okay but work through it.

The world does not evolve around your personal feelings or agenda. You must learn how to deal with bitter and sweet moments resulting in character building. In the parable, a job description was given and certain results were expected from the owner in his absence. It is not that important for you to like every assignment or every person in your life, but it is very important for you to be faithful, display wisdom, and show compassion at all times. For every assignment given, there is a day of reckoning.

29. The Barren Fig Tree
(Luke 13:6-9)

Comments

Once again, let us be mindful that parables are colorful and insightful stories relating to ethical, practical and spiritual concerns regarding the Kingdom of God. Jesus also used these parables as means of declaring divine judgment upon the religious leaders and others.

We will explore a short and popular parable, wherein Jesus used a fig tree to convey a spiritual truth. Obviously, the planter expected a harvest from his investment. However, the tree that failed to produce depicts a waste of space and time and does not deserve to continue existing. Either you produce (in worship and service), or you will face the consequences inherent in divine judgment. There are similar accounts of the fig tree throughout the Gospel (Matthew 3:10, 7:19; Matthew 21:18-20; Matthew 24:32:35; Mark 11:12-14, 20-21; Mark 3:10; Mark 7:19 and Luke 3:9).

1. What are the circumstances surrounding the origin of this parable?

A group of people approached Jesus regarding a massacre of Galileans ordered by King Pilate. It is suggested this may have been the group led by Judas of Galilee (Acts 5:37) because they constantly rebelled against Caesar's authority and refused to pay taxes. They went on to mention another devastation permeating around the Tower of Siloam (area in Jerusalem) and the untimely deaths of those nearby. Jesus responded to their concerns by making sure they understood suffering comes in many forms, but it is paramount they understood the importance of dying in the faith. Therefore, Jesus declared, "Unless you repent, you will all likewise perish."

2. Who is the parable addressed to?

Based upon the opening verse, it appears Jesus is speaking to the multitude.

3. What is the subject drawn from?

- The parable is drawn from a scene in nature.

- Fig trees were common throughout Israel and places along the Mediterranean Sea as they were staples of their daily diets.

- The New Testament terms *Suke/Sukea* refer to fig trees. This tree usually ripens in late May or early June.

4. Variations in the Gospels.

- The illustration in this parable is found only in Luke. Nonetheless, it serves as a wake-up call for Israel. God summoned her to a state of righteousness and holiness.

- Jesus dramatized this message by illustrating a man planting a fig tree in his vineyard. Planting a vineyard is strategic and suggests the need for cultivation and safeguarding versus a tree growing elsewhere unattended.

- Eventually, the man came looking for figs during the season but found none.

- The owner said to the vinedresser (attendant), "It has been three years, (rebirth/regeneration) and yet this tree continues to disappoint me."

- The owner instructs the vinedresser (attendant) to cut it down; it is useless.

- The vinedresser respectfully requested that the owner give him more time to cultivate and work with the tree.

- Both owner and vinedresser agreed to be gracious for another year. Either, the tree will produce, or it will be cut down the following year.

5. What applications can we make for our lives?

Without question, the parable spoke specifically to the spiritual realities of Israel. Alternatively, I see similar situations in the Church today. Christ has equipped His body with Spiritual Gifts of Grace; whereby, she can produce fruit of righteousness. However, in many instances, we see matured trees lacking production and filled with excuses. The Church represents the vineyard destined to bring forth fruit and give glory to Christ in this dispensation of Grace. We cannot afford to allow self-righteousness, traditions, rituals, denominations, societies, families, and finances push us into the soils of being unproductive.

6. Can you tell the story in your own words?

Jesus masterfully demonstrates how each of you will be held accountable for your actions. Either you put up or shut up (figuratively speaking) when it comes to the Kingdom of God. The vinedresser represents a Disciple, Ambassador or Believer in Christ who stands up for others, even though they may not be doing what they should be doing from time to time.

We must display patience and help cultivate the soil of the soul in our brothers and sisters. However, there comes a time when patience and expectation will run its due course. You are ultimately responsible for your own actions and decisions you make in life.

Figs are delightful and nutritious fruit, and so shall it be for all those who are planted in the vineyard of holiness. I urge you to bring forth the fruit of righteousness, or next year, you may be cut down (judgment). It is interesting that this parable does not reveal the final outcome for the tree. Likewise, it is up to you to write or factor in a favorable outcome.

30. The Lesson on Humility
(Luke 14:7-14)

Comments

Initially, this parable was not included in this compilation, and in many instances, it seems to be overshadowed by the one that follows: *The Parable of the Great Banquet.* Jesus is giving another perspective about the Kingdom of God permeating around humility.

Each of you must safeguard his or her self from being pre-occupied with status or placed in the seat of honor. Furthermore, Jesus teaches us about a spiritual mandate that includes the disinherited or even less-fortunate versus those who are familiar, or considered prominent in the community. The Kingdom of God is all-inclusive or universally for both: "the haves and have nots". Let us explore the nature of people seeking to be recognized or honored in public.

1. What are the circumstances surrounding the origin of this parable?

Jesus led His disciples into Jerusalem, the seat of the religious and political capital of Israel. It marks the final stage of His earthly ministry on the Sabbath Day in the home of a Pharisee and in the presence of other community leaders. Interestingly, Jesus wanted to know from these leaders, if was it lawful to heal a man diagnosed with dropsy on this holy day. They refused to answer as a result of detecting this as an incriminating question. Thus,

Jesus seized the opportunity to teach what was most important in these situations.

2. Who is the parable addressed to?

The parable is addressed to the religious leaders obsessed in self-righteousness, selfish motives, and recognition.

3. What is the subject drawn from?

- This parable is drawn from a common experience; the seating arrangements at this wedding feast will teach all of us a lesson in humility.

- The New Testament term *Gamos* denotes marriage or marriage feast. Marriage is the sacred institution, wherein we experience the union or covenant between a man and woman, but is also consummated and witnessed by family and friends.

- The *Seat of Honor* from ancient times was preserved for prominent members within the community, and people are usually escorted to these reserved seats.

- The term *humility* derives from the New Testament word *tuperinophrosune.* It denotes lowliness of mind, abased, or low degree.

4. Variations in the Gospels.

- This parable is found only in Luke and is followed by another parable in verse 16.

- Jesus draws our attention to what is really important versus that which is less important by utilizing the illustration of an invited guest list.

- Societies throughout the world have recognized varying degrees of social status.

- It is best to not assume one should be in the front, even though you may have a prestigious title. Therefore, it is best to be ushered to your seat upon entering.

- Apparently, there were guests who took the liberty to seat themselves in reserved areas not meant for them.

- This poor choice brought embarrassment to them when they were asked to move elsewhere. This illustration depicts the lifestyle of the Pharisees.

- Verse 10 demonstrates how you should behave as an invited guest. It is best to sit toward the rear or the outer circle than to place yourself in the seat of honor, so that the host may ask you to move to a more prestigious place.

- The term exalt derives from the New Testament word *Hupsoo* and means to lift up or being raised. Self-exaltation is a derivative of Satan; however, all those who are humble or submit his or her self will be exalted by the Lord. This statement is a paradox that appears as a contradiction but displays a profound truth in the end.

- Verse 12 challenges the Pharisee who invited Jesus to consider their traditional views. People in general tend to invite family, friends, or prominent (rich) individuals to a wedding. It is like someone doing something with the expectation of being rewarded.

- Verse 13 gives us a new perspective regarding the kingdom. Even the poor have a right to aesthetics and happiness; therefore, they too should be invited to the wedding feast or any public setting, even though they cannot afford to or may be an embarrassment to you.

5. What applications can we make for our lives?

It should be the Church's aim to please Christ and esteem His Lordship as opposed to seeking fame and honor. It is not a sin to be honored and recognized based upon your service to humanity, but please permit honor to occur, while maintaining a spirit of humility at all times.

6. Can you tell the story in your own words?

The marriage feast is a figurative way of describing the Church being united with Christ. The great and gracious host is Jesus Christ, along with the angels. Believers in Christ should not concern themselves with recognition, promotions, or places of honor. There is more than enough room at the Lord's feast for all of us. The mere fact that you are invited should be enough to cause you to be thankful. An invitation is an extension or a welcome to attend an important event.

Despite this enlightening parable, we do not see any indication the religious leaders perceived they were the focus or target of this illustration. You will always end up in the favorable place in the Kingdom of God if you remain humble.

31. The Great Supper
(Luke 14:16-24)

Comments

We are moving toward the end of the parables recorded in the Gospel. The Kingdom of God was introduced in a profound and welcoming manner by Jesus, and therein lies both the mystery and truth as it relates to reconciliation with God.

In this parable, we are about to explore what happened when a select group (Hebrew Israelites) was invited to a great feast. However, each invited guest had an excuse and refused to attend. Remember, this was not a casual evening dinner, but one that was well planned.

Their refusal disappointed the Master/Householder. Nonetheless, the event would not be cancelled, but rather other guests would replace them. Therefore, he summoned his servants to go and find men and women from the least expected places and reputations (reflecting the universal Church), and tell them to come to the supper.

On several occasions, Jesus shared similar teachings, wherein invited guests responded, inappropriately. Spiritually speaking, it is in your best interest to accept and drop what you are doing when you receive an invitation from the Lord. At any rate, we will see their poor choices will not circumvent the fellowship ordained by God.

1. What are the circumstances surrounding the origin of this parable?

Jesus has entered Jerusalem on the Sabbath Day as He is ushering in the final days of His ministry. This chapter opens by, once again, placing Him in the home of a Pharisee. In effect, there are two parables in this chapter relating to religious leaders' inquiry on what is lawful. The parable also illustrates the broad-minded and inclusive ministry of the Messiah. Furthermore, they seemed to have great concerns about positioning or status when it comes to important events. In other words, religious leaders were trying to entrap or trick Jesus.

2. Who is the parable addressed to?

The parable is addressed specifically to religious leaders who were preoccupied with protocol. However, the parable is applicable to the multitude and disciples who were nearby.

3. What is the parable drawn from?

- The parable is drawn from a common experience, namely *The Great Supper.*

- The New Testament term *Deipnon* denotes supper. This term refers to a feast or festival shared by a large group or people at the end of the day. It was a time to fellowship.

- Generally speaking, Israel celebrated three major feast (Exodus 23:14-17).

4. Variations in the Gospels.

- This parable is found only in Luke.

- Verse 15 reminds us these teachings relate to the Kingdom of God. A person is blessed if he or she partakes in this spiritual feast and also learns from this earthly illustration.

- The parable presents a man who hosted a great banquet and invited various guests based upon relationships or someone he knew.

- Invitations are usually earmarked for family, friends, community leaders, or respectable persons.

- The Master sent his servant to announce and invite guests to the feast.

- We will observe three men giving legitimate excuses and they are as followed:

- **I have bought a field**. Based upon Hebraic customs, a man had a legal right to inspect property/field prior to consummating a contract. Therefore, the man felt comfortable giving his excuse and rejecting the invitation.

- **I have bought 5 yokes of oxen.** Once again, Hebraic customs allowed the purchaser the right to try out the oxen prior to finalizing the transaction. Therefore, he too felt comfortable giving an excuse and not attend the feast.

- **I have married a wife.** Based upon Mosaic Laws (Deuteronomy 24:5), a man was exempt from the military and other societal duties for one year after marriage. Therefore, he had no problem refusing the invitation.

- The servant returned to the Master and shared the report of each individual.

- The Master is very disappointed, but focused on the issue at hand because there cannot be a feast without a large gathering.

- Therefore, the Master instructed the servant to go to the streets, lanes, alleys, or places nearby and **bring** (not invited) the poor, maimed, blind, and lame etc.

- Based upon conventional thinking, the religious leaders and respectable people would not factor in this population at a feast of this magnitude.

- The servant came back and told the Master he had fulfilled the request, but there was room for more.

- The Master really knew the purpose of a feast, so he sent the servant out again to the outer areas, highways, and hedges, but this time **compelled** them to come to the feast.

- Lastly, Jesus reminded us in verse 24 that even if the invited guests were to change their minds, they would not be accepted to the feast.

5. What applications can we make for our lives?

We live in an era where there seems to be a bombardment of celebrations, but these activities are not necessarily spiritual or wholesome in nature. Biblically speaking, a feast permeates around something sacred or a memorial due to being keenly aware it was the Lord's Goodness that allowed the same to be established. For example, Church Anniversary, Family Reunion, Birthday, and Retirement usually is carried out based upon invitations. Generally speaking, you may wonder why and be disappointed when an invited guest fails to attend. However, in this parable, the Master wasted no time with those who sent excuses, but rather got replacements in order for the feast to go on as scheduled.

6. Can you tell the story in your own words?

Jesus was truly a Master Teacher. In many instances, we find ourselves sitting around like the religious leaders trying to position themselves in esteemed positions. Fellowship is germane to the Kingdom of God, but it cannot be restricted to our personal invitation list. The parable goes on to illustrate the inclusive and creative nature of God: namely invitations bringing and compelling people to come. Even further, we cannot afford to present any excuses when it comes to kingdom ministry. When the call is made, you must respond accordingly and handle mundane matters, later. It does not matter when or how you get into the Supper but make sure you are not left out.

32. Tower and King Making War
(Luke 14:25-35)

Comments

This marks the third parable in the chapter. Jesus is making it abundantly clear the Kingdom of God was carefully planned. The title for this parable is appropriate, but could equally be labeled, *Conditions of Discipleship.*

We are about to examine what appears to be a controversial statement predicated upon family relationships and a divine calling. But in truth, these statements are designed to make you ponder over what is most important in life. We will observe Jesus utilizing an illustration pertaining to what is the appropriate way to construct a tower as well as the inappropriate way a king should go to war. Even further, Jesus will share a metaphor on salt in order for us to comprehend the effective nature or spirit inherent in all those who adhere to the Gospel of the Kingdom.

1. What are the circumstances surrounding the origin of this parable?

Jesus appears to be in the same place when we discussed the Great Supper.

2. Who is the parable addressed to?

According to verse 25, Jesus is speaking specifically to the multitude surrounding Him and the religious leaders nearby.

3. What is the subject drawn from?

- This parable is drawn from common experiences, namely the tower construction and a king preparing for war.

- The New Testament term *Purgos* denotes a tower. Generally speaking, it refers to a watchtower overseeing a vineyard. For the most part, they were built upon sizeable stones.

- The Old Testament term *Melek* and New Testament term *Basileus* refer to a king. A king serves as a sovereign ruler, displays royalty, and implements justice entrusted with final authority in the kingdom. The model King throughout Israel's history was David, who embodied praise, worship, holiness, and righteousness.

- The term *War* in scripture is a confrontation between two forces. Although wars are clearly noted throughout the Bible, it is not the ideal or ultimate means of resolving conflict.

4. Variations in the Gospels.

- This parable is found only in Luke.

- Verse 25 places Jesus in the midst of the crowd in Jerusalem.

- The use of the term *hate* derives from the Greek word *Miseo*. In this case, Jesus is simply reminding us we cannot serve two masters. Under no circumstances do we see Jesus urging anyone to be antagonistic toward family. However, due to the examples of righteousness and unrighteousness in the world, there will be division and choices made.

- There is a cost for discipleship and a choice for embracing righteousness or succumbing to unrighteousness.

- Verse 27 makes reference to the Cross of Calvary and serves as a reminder there will be public shame and humiliation for the disciple who faithfully follows Jesus.

- Verse 28 speaks about a tower that was apparently nearby and used in reference to the Kingdom of God.

- Constructing a tower entails planning, organized labor, patience, and sacrifice. He cautioned the listeners they should not underestimate the overall cost for completing the project.

- Mockery and ridicule is associated with unfinished projects, such as the nearby tower that was not completed. However, there should be no misunderstanding by thinking the shame associated with the cross defeated the message from the Kingdom of God.

- Jesus moves on to another parable by referring to a king preparing for a war. Historically, we cannot parallel this statement with a war in and around Jerusalem at the time.

- Prior to launching an attack or defending the territory, a wise king should consult his advisors or counselors in order to determine the sufficient number of troops as well as determine if war is appropriate.

- In some instances, wisdom may prevail in surrendering and avoiding a blood bath within the kingdom.

- In both cases, tower and war, Jesus reminds us that there must be all or none when it comes to being a follower or disciple.

- Jesus concludes this chapter by calling upon the salt mineral, to illustrate its useful purpose on earth. This metaphor reminds us of the penetrating and preserving taste of salt. Either the salt will carry out her purpose, or be thrown away. The reference to salt also serves as a reminder of the covenant or spiritual seasoning associated with God's Chosen people, Israel.

5. What applications can we make for our lives?

This parable sets forth an opportunity for each of you to take advantage of planning and being committed to a very important goal. Let me give an illustration. On one hand, I recognize President George Bush's commitment to the War in Iraq. Alternatively, his military advisors misled him because there was no exit plan. Spiritually speaking, it is imperative for you to make up your mind and turn your heart over to God and stop playing church.

6. Can you tell the story in your own words?

Jesus masterfully used these parables to ignite the consciousness of all those surrounding Him. "Bad things can and will happen to good people," but in the final analysis, it all boils down to the choices you make. If you fall short in your spiritual calculation (sin), there is no one to fault but yourself. It is important to allow yourself to be preserved with the *Savior's Salt;* it is the nature of Satan to present alternatives for you to fall short.

We must remain humble and dedicated to a life of grace and mercy as opposed to arrogance and pride. A prayerful and consecrated life will help ensure you to have more than enough once the construction is underway, or you have to confront the enemy in a war. But at all costs, do not find yourself being useless, wherein the Master will have to throw you away like the salt that had lost its savor?

33. The Lost Coin
(Luke 15:8-10)

Comments

It is important we do not lose sight regarding the purpose of parables in the New Testament. The term *parable* derives from the Greek word *Parabole.* Generally speaking, it denotes placing beside, lay aside, or to compare. Jesus' use of parables is designed to unlock the mysteries surrounding the Kingdom of God.

This chapter introduced three unique perspectives focusing on retrieving what is lost: *lost sheep, lost coin, & lost son.* For now, we are focusing on the second parable: Lost Coin. It is relatively short, but yet meaningful. We will explore a woman who, more than likely, was a widow who lost her meager possession: a silver coin.

I have written a sermon surrounding these parables, which goes into greater detail in highlighting the reason, in each case, for being lost. Let us examine how this woman failed to **pay close attention** to her funds, thus resulting in it being lost. Even further, Disciples of Christ must be vigilant and faithful at all times to the teachings of the Kingdom of God, or they too will find themselves lost in a world of sin.

1. What are the circumstances surrounding the origin of this parable?

It appears Jesus is moving throughout Jerusalem. On one hand, the multitude is following Him (14:25). On the other hand, we know the religious leaders are curious to entrap Him regarding His teachings (14:1; 15:1) and seized every moment to ask tricky questions.

2. Who is the parable addressed to?

According to verse two, Jesus is addressing the Pharisees, who seemed to be taking issue with Him intermingling with the Tax Collectors or sinners. Thus, He is speaking specifically to the religious leaders.

3. What is the subject drawn from?

- This parable is drawn from a common experience, namely a mission coin.

- The coin is referred to as a piece of silver, a valuable commodity, and served as the primary currency for exchange in Israel. In other words, it had great value.

- The Greek term *Drachmen* denotes the 4th part of a shekel (1/2 oz.).

4. Variations in the Gospels.

- This parable is found only in Luke.

- Jesus highlighted a woman who had lost one of her coins within the house due to her negligence.

- She searched diligently by herself until she finds it. This illustration serves as a reminder that none of you are too far from God, but you must put forth the effort.

- The woman could not afford to lose 10% of her revenue.

- Eventually, she found the coin and later called her friends and neighbors to celebrate.

- Jesus draws a parallel with the retrieving of the lost coin to persons or sinners adhering to the Gospel of the Kingdom.

- The heavens rejoice, namely God and the angels, when you are awakened by this eternal message and enter the Kingdom of God.

5. What applications can we make for our lives?

Each of you must view your journey through life as a unique opportunity to worship and serve creatively. More specifically, you should safeguard the eternal message embedded in the Gospel of the Kingdom. Paying close attention to important matters will serve as your link to happiness or unhappiness.

For example, there was a mass killing on the campus of Virginia Tech University in 2007. It turns out the young shooter; a Korean, had emotional and psychological problems. Obviously, his family, friends, and colleagues did not pay close attention to his signs of illness. The lack of paying attention to wholesome advice can result in being lost and feeling uncomfortable. Metaphorically speaking, the term *lost* derives from the Greek word *Appolumi* meaning failing to be saved or perishing due to sin.

6. Can you tell the story in your own words?

This is a straightforward parable that clearly reminds us how tangible and how valuable things can get away from you. The silver coin did not lose itself, but rather, it was due to carelessness and the lack of paying attention.

Some people might simply write off a 10% loss, but she could not afford to do so. Let me assume you love God, but have you lost your patience, joy, love, and peace? The single, silver coin belonged to the widow that could produce greater value in the company of other coins. Each of us in our singleness or detachment cannot be very effective. It is the nature of Satan to distract us and become careless in the area of spiritual concerns. However, Jesus makes it clear there is joy in heaven over one sinner (someone lost) when there is a change of heart/mind (repent), and the return to your rightful place in the Kingdom of God.

34. The Lost Son(s)
(Luke 15:11-32)

Comments

We have reached the 34th parable preserved in the Gospel of the Kingdom. Each of these parables revealed the hidden nature inherent in the kingdom and waiting for you to discover. Therefore, these stories are placed alongside concrete realities as opposed to myths, fables, or romanticized versions of reality. In short, they are here for you to discover the truth.

This marks the 3rd longest and last parable in chapter 15. Traditionally, this story is commonly called *The Prodigal Son.* Once you read and observe this account, it becomes rather obvious that a lost soul is very important in relation to the kingdom. However, if you take an even closer look at the story, you will see that both sons were lost and needed reconciliation with the Father.

The basis of the younger son being lost is hinged upon rebellion, arrogance, and prideful. Furthermore, we will observe the son who remained home was lost in religion or self-entitlement. The teaching on being lost serves as a reminder that someone is operating outside the favor (Grace) of God.

1. What are the circumstances surrounding the origin of this parable?

In this previous parable, *The Lost Coin,* we observed Jesus in Jerusalem being challenged by the religious leaders.

2. Who is the parable addressed to?

Jesus is addressing concerns raised by the Pharisees.

3. What is the parable drawn from?

- This parable is drawn from a common experience, based upon the actions of the sons.

- The term *son* stems from the Old Testament word *Ben* and New Testament term *Huios.* In both cases, they refer to a descendant or offspring. Metaphorically it is associated with the following phrases in scripture: *Son of God; Son of Man; Son of Perdition; Sons of Light; Sons of Evil* and *Sons of Disobedience.* As you can see, it is a relational term.

4. Variations in the Gospels.

- This parable is found only in Luke.

- Jesus shares a story about a father, and although the mother is not mentioned, be assured she is in the background. The family had two sons and lived on a large estate.

- The younger son showed disrespect by asking the father to give him the portion of properties due him.

According to cultural values and the scriptures, this normally occurred as a directive of the father or after his demise (Deuteronomy 21:16-21).

- Nonetheless, we observe the wisdom of the father, and perhaps the urging of the mother in the background toward granting the younger son's request.

- Subsequently, the young man left with a sizeable amount of properties: food, livestock, money, and perhaps servants.

- He traveled and ended up in a foreign place far from home.

- Eventually, he lost all his possessions. Meanwhile, God caused a famine to occur where he was living. The Old Testament term *Raab* denotes a lack of food displayed over a vast area for a prolonged period of time. It is best to never say it cannot get any worse.

- He became desperate for food and income. Therefore, one of the foreigners directed him to engage in a humiliating chore, feeding swine.

- The mere fact he was associated in any form with swine served as the culminating indignity for a Hebrew.

- It got so bad; he was prepared to eat the same food as the swine; none of his *so-called friends* shared their resources with him.

- Eventually, this humiliating experience caused him to wake up (awareness) and reflect on the abundance within his father's household. Therefore, he decided it was time to return home.

- This rebellious son came to his senses and basically said, I will confess my faults and ask my father to forgive me. He was willing to be reduced to the status of a servant and no longer be recognized as a son.

- He made up his mind and started the journey back home. The father recognized his son and was moved with compassion to forget what happened in the past while a distance, away. Of course, in my personal opinion, I believe the mother (representing grace) was in the background urging him along.

- The father graciously received the younger, lost son by embracing and kissing him.

- On one hand, the son is repenting while the father is restoring him as a son by giving him a robe, ring, and shoes. Each of these items distinguished a son versus a servant within the household.

- In the spirit of fellowship (*koinonia*), a calf was killed and a feast prepared.

- The celebration permeated around a son who was lost (transgressed) and perhaps presumed dead. He was lost and found dead in trespasses, but he was made alive, now.

- In verse 25, we observe the elder son on the scene who took note of the celebration. Please remember, this son had remained faithful to the father and family values while never leaving home.

- He called one of the servants and asked for an explanation.

- The servant enthusiastically told him about the return of his younger brother.

- Upon hearing the news, he became very angry and refused to enter the house and join the celebration.

- The father is made aware of the elder son's attitude and behavior. Then, he goes outside to address his elder son's concerns.

- The elder son reminded the father of his loyalty by never disobeying him or leaving home, but the elder son had never been given a celebration in his honor.

- He went on to say you did all this for your rebellious son, who defamed your name, as soon as he returned home.

- Once again, the wisdom of the father stands out by calling him son. He goes on to teach kingdom principles by reminding him everything here has been, is, and shall be yours because that is the nature of inheritance.

- The father goes on to remind him it was appropriate to forgive, welcome, and celebrate the return of your brother because he has been restored to his rightful place.

5. What applications can we make for our lives?

It is in the nature of Satan to cause separation either through pride or self-righteousness. Daily, I observe families torn apart due to shallow thoughts and selfish reasons. This parable serves as a reminder that it appeared to be a 50% lost (Prodigal Son) initially, but we take note of the elder son's behavior. We actually see a 100% loss in the household. Both, the behavior of the younger and elder sons prompted the father to reach out to them.

6. Can you tell the story in your own words?

In the younger son's case, he clearly disrespected his father and the traditional values of the community. Subsequently, God allowed him to realize his mistakes and repent. Alternatively, the elder son was expected to know better (like church folks), but he was too caught up in self-righteousness until he was blinded to the truth right at his fingertips.

Instead of rejoicing about the return of his younger brother, he was enraged in jealousy. The father displayed wisdom, received the younger son, and forgave him. Moreover, the father tried to teach the older son, but the parable concludes without telling us whether or not he accepted the father's explanation. Each of you must safeguard your mind against pride and arrogance because they will cause you to make foolish mistakes in life. Likewise, you must never think you are entitled to salvation. All the provisions within the Kingdom of God are there because of God's grace and love.

35. The Unjust Judge
(Luke 16:1-13)

Comments

The use of parables are effective teaching tools simply because they give us insights into spiritual, ethical, and practical concerns that would remain hidden, otherwise. Jesus masters the art of storytelling, and we have a clearer picture of the Kingdom of God because of these illustrations.

This parable draws a unique parallel between the spiritual and material aspects of life. On one hand, the righteous are given wealth and prosperity as a means to a greater good, while he/she is encouraged to not serve money or become entrapped with materialism. Jesus equates the love for money with the service of mammon.

This parable unlocks the difference in wealth utilized on behalf of the Kingdom of God versus wealth utilized for selfish reasons. The following New Testament scriptures will shed some light on the appropriate or righteous use of money (Matthew 3:11-12, 5:27-30, 6:19-24, 19:21-26; Mark 1:8, 10:21-27; Luke 3:16-17, 12:13-15, 12:33-34, 18:22-27). In far too many instances, people seem to never be satisfied with their possessions, but often discover they were poor managers in what they had already been assigned.

1. What are the circumstances surrounding the origin of this parable?

In the previous chapter, Jesus was seen in the midst of the Publicans and Tax Collectors. This parable does not indicate if he has left that place or continues to teach in the same place. At any rate, Jesus deemed it necessary to set the record straight on the appropriate and inappropriate use of money.

2. Who is the parable addressed to?

The chapter opens by mentioning Jesus was speaking specifically to the disciples.

3. What is the subject drawn from?

The parable is drawn from a common experience.

- The New Testament Greek term for *steward* is *Oikonmos* . It denotes the manager of a household or estate (oikos = house and *nemos* = to arrange).

- The term *accused* derives from the Greek word *Aitia.* It refers to a charge, case, or fault launched against someone by an official.

- The term *mammon* stems from an Aramaic word *Mamonas.* The term has to do with treasurers or riches trusted to someone.

4. Variations in the Gospels.

- This parable is found only in Luke, however, there are other stories relating to stewardship (see outline).

- Jesus begins this parable by telling the disciples about a rich man who entrusted the business affairs of his estate to a steward for a certain length of time.

- Charges were launched against the steward for wasting or mishandling the goods at the estate. It is obvious the steward did not expect the owner to return when he did and asked to give an account.

- The owner summoned the steward and demanded a full report, and the owner stripped the steward of his duties because he lost confidence in him.

- The steward is ashamed and had to accept this ruling. However, he began to think what he shall do in this state of reality.

- Eventually, he eliminated various options such as not physically able to dig and too proud to beg. Always remember, any flaw in your character will eventually come out if it is present.

- The unjust steward decides to make plans for the future (of course, without the owner's permission) regarding income.

- He went to the owner's debtors and worked out a deal with each, so that in the future, they would be gracious toward him.

- One man owed the owner 100 measurers of oil, but he only requested him to pay 50% of the debt.

- Another man owed the owner 100 measurers of wheat, but he only requested him to pay 80% of the debt.

- After a while, the owner is made aware of these transactions and actually lauded and praised him for his business savvy. Jesus went on to draw a parallel between the *Sons of the World* and the *Sons of Light.* And so it is in life, there are good and bad characters.

- The Sons of Light were supposed to be spiritually enlightened (John 12:36; Ephesians 5:8; 1 Thessalonians 5:5 and the Dead Sea Scrolls). In essence, Jesus is saying those who have been redeemed should know how to handle the affairs of the Kingdom of God in a similar manner like the steward.

- Jesus goes on to teach the disciples how to understand the full benefit or purpose behind the mammon (Malachi 3:10 and 1 Corinthians 16:2).

- Verses 10-13 serves as a commentary on the contrasting characters or behaviors expressed in people throughout all generations.

- Faithfulness and honesty does not discriminate, just like drugs and alcohol. A person can be responsible or irresponsible with little and much.

- Mammon refers to temporal treasurers, but Jesus seems to be saying failure to manage your funds in this sphere entails you likely will do the same, spiritually (verse 11).

- The unjust steward failed to properly manage the owner's estate; however, he would have also benefitted if he had taken care of the owner.

- Jesus concludes this parable by challenging the disciples and those surrounding Him to choose sides as to whom you will serve in this life (Matthew 6:33 & Proverbs 3:5-6).

5. What applications can we make for our lives?

A report in the local news conveyed City of Milwaukee Employees were using their time while on the clock, inappropriately. It went on to report several employees were caught on camera taking excessive breaks and parked in unauthorized places. You are accountable for your actions and management of your time.

You have been entrusted with life, talents, time, resources, and abilities for a season. Ask yourself, have I failed to be faithful and honest on things I initially agreed to manage? There are consequences for your actions. It may seem as if you are getting away with something, the truth is there is a day of reckoning coming sooner, or later.

6. Can you tell the story in your own words?

I marvel at the way Jesus selected specific stories to compliment the message at hand. There is definitely a spiritual hierarchy operating in the universe. It does not matter if you are an employer or employee, we are all under authority. Sooner or later, the true owner of heaven and earth will summon each of us to give an account of stewardship. The analysis of the Sons of Light versus the Sons of the World serves as a reminder you should be prudent over affairs assigned to you and never operate deceitfully.

There is no excuse or sympathy for the unjust steward because the owner had confidence in him to do what was responsible in his presence or absence. God is counting on you to handle the affairs of His kingdom in a responsible (not wasteful) manner. Divine judgment is inevitable, although we live in a dispensation of Grace. The parable illustrates the steward was stripped of his title and expelled from the estate due to his actions.

If you serve Satan and this world, you can only expect temporal benefits. Alternatively, when you serve on behalf of the Kingdom of God, it incorporates both the temporal and eternal blessings of the Most High God.

Lastly, when you handle your business properly, there must be an investment set aside for the future or the unforeseen challenges that lie ahead. The character of the steward was inappropriate, but Jesus deemed it necessary to draw an analogy from the examples of compassion, mercy, and forgiveness regarding debts while conducting business.

37. The Rich Man and Lazarus
(Luke 16:19-31)

Comments

Jesus was profound in His teachings and parables which played a significant role. These stories were unique and insightful, but more importantly, they helped unlocked the mysteries surrounding the Kingdom of God.

This parable is widely used in the church and may be labeled a classic. It draws a clear parallel between a man with wealth and a man with wants. It is amazing to see the behavior of people with tremendous resources failing to be sensitive and compassionate toward someone who was desperate.

From antiquity, there have been classes or social statuses among people, and be assured this reality will continue. Nonetheless, Jesus makes it crystal clear that each of you will be judged after this life based upon the principles set forth in the Kingdom of God. Remember, it is not a sin to have wealth and riches, but you must watch your character and attitude when it comes to what you have and what others may need. We will observe this serves as the longest parable.

1. **What are the circumstances surrounding the origin of this parable?**

The Pharisees were notorious for challenging Jesus (Luke 16:14). In this case, they had an unrighteous appetite for wealth. In the previous parable, Jesus talked about the unjust steward, and now He is amongst religious leaders with the intent of shedding some light on the appropriate use of money and helping others who are less fortunate.

2. Who is the parable addressed to?

This parable is addressed to religious leaders with a distorted perspective regarding wealth and prosperity.

3. What is the parable drawn from?

The parable is drawn from a common experience, namely the rich and poor man.

- The term *rich* derive from the Greek nouns *Ploutos & Euporia.* They denote abundance, having plenty, or being prosperous.
- The term *poor* derived from the Old Testament word *Ani.* It refers to being weak, afflicted, or humble. The New Testament term *Ptochos* refers to a beggar or someone who is depraved of essential needs.

4. Variations in the Gospels.

- This parable is found only in Luke.
- Jesus shared a story about a rich man (Latin term *Dives)* who lived lavishly in purple (royalty) clothing, fine linen, and ate exceptionally well every day.
- There are wealthy people who choose not to be extravagant like Dives.

- In contrast to the rich man, there was also a poor man named Lazarus.
- Lazarus is the Hellenized (Greek) variation of the Hebrew name *Eleazar* which basically means *God need helpers*.
- Interestingly and unique to Luke's writing, Jesus saw fit to mention the name of the poor beggar.
- The poor man represented a reoccurring reality in the community that often goes ignored. The poor man was positioned at the entrance of the rich man's estate, so there could be no excuse in not seeing the need.
- In contrast to the accessories of the rich man, we observe Lazarus described with sores and a desire to eat the crumbs or left over from the rich man's table. Without mentioning it, we can assume he was malnourished and sickly due to a lack of food.
- God always has a plan when you fail to cooperate. Therefore, God directed the dogs to lick the wounds in order to provide some form of relief from his misery.
- Eventually, we see an interruption: divine judgment with the demise of Lazarus. This also served as relief from his misery.
- After his demise, Lazarus is escorted into the bosom of the legendary father of the faith: Abraham. This is a metaphoric phrase that also sheds light into the doctrines of the hereafter or heaven from a Jewish perspective. Furthermore, it represents a place of blessing along with a position of honor.

- In addition to the poor man's death, we are told the rich man also died, and this illustrates death does not discriminate. All of us will die, and it is best to make preparation for her.
- To some, death is seen as the final interruption, but in truth there are activities beyond death and the grave this parable illuminates.
- The rich man had a proper or ceremonial burial, but there is no mentioning of a burial for the poor man, Lazarus.
- There was a contrast in the physical life regarding the rich and poor. Likewise, there is a contrast after death between Heaven and Hades.
- The rich man ended up in a place called Hades. Scripturally and traditionally speaking, it referred to a temporary region of departed spirits of the lost (but including the blessed dead in the period preceding the ascension of Christ). It seems to have a different function from Sheol, Gehenna, and Hell.
- While in Hades, Dives beheld Abraham consoling Lazarus, but they were at a distance. This reality caused him to call out to Abraham, but to no avail.
- He went on to ask mercifully for Lazarus, whom he previously neglected, to dip his finger in some water to cool his tongue. However, Abraham reminded him that he was where he was due to the bad choices he made on the other side of life.
- Abraham was like an Archetype of Christ, and he went on to remind him about the pleasurable life he lived on earth and the evil (bad) life experienced by Lazarus. However, in the next life, we saw a shift in

treatment and status. The rich is tormented and the poor, comforted.

- Jesus further illustrates there is a gulf or great divide between the righteous and the unrighteous. There is no crossing over on either sides, and your residence is permanent upon arrival.
- The rich man was relentless in his pleas for mercy. After he realized there was no deliverance or escape, he appealed to Abraham (father) to send Lazarus to his five brothers, who apparently were displaying a similar lifestyle.
- Once again, we observe no redemption beyond the grave. Abraham reminded him God had sent Moses and the Prophets for them to listen and obey.
- He continues his plead by saying, "If someone goes to them from the grave, they will repent."
- Once again and finally, Abraham makes it clear God has sent messengers of reconciliation throughout all generations. If the people failed to hear the messengers of God, then there will be no sensational account of hearing and seeing someone from the grave or spirit world.

5. What applications can we make for our lives?

Looking at the sovereignty of God, there are certain aspects of His reign we continue to struggle with or seek understanding. For example, a United Nations Report reveals 60% of the world population lives off $2.00 per day, and this includes families. Why do you suppose this reality exists while there are adequate resources for everyone? Yes, it, realizing the majority of goods and services are in the hands of less than 5% of the population is a bitter pill to swallow.

In my humble opinion, poverty, economic exploitation, corruption, malnutrition, and poor education etc. exist because of policies. It is not a sin to be wealthy, but it is a sin to display greed, pride, and selfishness at the expense of the poor and disinherited. None of you should envy for what others have, but it is appropriate to ask for help from those with resources. Even further, we must come to grips with the reality that Lazarus's condition never changed on earth but was rewarded in Heaven.

6. Can you tell the story in your own words?

During a spring revival, 2007 Heritage International Ministries, Dr. James Powell shed light on the blessings disguised in the life of Lazarus. For example, he stated, "We can live off the crumbs and the dogs are there to lick the wounds of life."

Sometimes, we may find ourselves in desperate situations, wherein life does not seem to be fair. There will always be the scenario of a rich man and Lazarus on earth. A wealthy person who shares generously with others is wise, and he or she is making investments in the Kingdom of God. Furthermore, his or her behavior opens the door for perpetual blessings or curses.

Abraham is mentioned because he was spiritual, wealthy, generous, and tremendously blessed and not selfish like Dives. Abraham understood blessings come to pass along to others. Lazarus is mentioned because he represented a missed opportunity although it was disguised in poverty. The religious leaders claimed to be rich in the Hebraic tradition alongside serving as the guardians of the sacred texts preserved in the Law (Torah) and Prophets (Nabi), but in truth, they were spiritually dead and detached, just like the rich man.

Lastly, there is nothing wrong having an abundance of material things, but you must remain humble. There should not be a gulf/division between the haves and have nots because God is the source of it all. After all, should one negate the family and childhood friends simply because you have arrived, and they may be experiencing misfortunes at the present time?

37. The Unprofitable Servant
(Luke 17:7-10)

Comments

There are those who choose not to treat this story as a parable. However, we think otherwise because it gives us another keen insight regarding the Kingdom of God.

This is a relatively short parable but just as meaningful as the lengthy ones. We will discover what it really means to have a faithful and obedient relationship with God. There are definite periods in our lives, wherein rewards are appropriate. However, Jesus deems it necessary to teach about the importance of awareness and being dutiful. A true servant makes no excuses about what they have already done, especially when there is work to be accomplished.

1. What are the circumstances surrounding the origin of this parable?

In the earlier verses of this chapter, Jesus referred to his followers as disciples (verse 1) and apostles (verse 5). One refers to being trained, while the other, administration. As disciples, he taught them temptations are inevitable. As apostles, they need to understand the value of faith. Therefore, the parable surfaced due to a lack of clarity as it relates to what is paramount in the Kingdom of God.

2. Who is the parable addressed to?

The parable is addressed specifically to the disciples, but on a larger scale it serves as a spiritual indictment against the religious leaders. Even further, it serves as an eye-opener for the multitude that was near.

3. What is the parable drawn from?

This parable is drawn from a common experience based upon the vocation and expectation of the servants in the household.

- The New Testament noun and verb for *servant* is *Doulos & Douloo.* They denote subjection or bondman. They also refer to ministering on behalf of someone in authority.

- Servants worked within the house or in the field.

- The New Testament term for *duty* is *Opheilo*. It refers to owing, doing what you ought to do, or being bound to perform.

4. Variations in the Gospels.

- This parable is found only in Luke.

- Jesus begins this story by asking a series of questions to his disciples.

- Agriculture (plowing) and domesticated animals (sheep) were very common in the area where Jesus ministered. Therefore, these realities assisted Jesus in making a point about the rule of a servant.

- Let us suppose a servant worked all day fulfilling his or her duties on the estate and returned to the house at the end of the day.

- Do you suppose the owner will invite him or her to sit at the table and dine with his family?

- Or does it seem more likely for the owner to assign or expect the servant to continue working, and this may include preparing dinner in order that his family may eat.

- It is appropriate for the servant to sit and dine after the owner and his family have been served and eaten.

- Jesus went on to ask the disciples in verse 9 if it was appropriate for the owner to thank the servant for doing his job, or was it simply expected of him to do so?

- Jesus concluded this parable by reminding the disciples they are also expected to fulfill a spiritual mandate in the kingdom without making excuses.

5. What applications can we make for our lives?

In the western value system, there seems to be some misunderstanding on the use of thanking an individual regarding certain tasks they perform. Please, allow me to explain because my parents taught us to always be hospitable coming from the south (Louisiana). However, looking from another perspective I see far too many people waiting to be *pat on the back* or receive accolades for things they were already expected to do.

For example, it is alright to thank me for assisting you change a flat tire. However, you do not need to thank me for showing up for work where a paycheck is also involved.   It is alright to thank members of the congregation for assisting me in a disaster relief project, but I should not have to thank members of the congregation for attending worship. My wife should not have to thank me for taking out the garbage or washing dishes.

There is a story that may assist in driving this point home. Once, there was a wealthy man who contributed one million dollars in the offering. Upon giving, he paused and turned to the pastor and said, "I thought you would have said thanks for the generous donation I gave?" The pastor responded, "He who gives should be thankful that he has something to give."

6. Can you tell the story in your own words?

Did Jesus need to thank the disciples for following Him, or should they have been thankful for deliverance from their old ways and becoming a follower of Christ? We live in a whining, complaining, and ungrateful world. I observe far too many days and celebrations of recognition occurring. Look around and see the conditions in our congregation,   community,   schools,   families,   and government. We need to revive our work ethics and stop behaving as if we are doing someone a favor because you are doing something noteworthy.

It is not a sin or inappropriate to thank someone for a good deed, but you are expected to worship and serve when you have already agreed to become a disciple or member of the covenant community.   Therefore, do not become disheartened when your name is not called upon for special recognition.

As long as we breathe God's air and walk the earth, He has provided, and you ought to be thankful. From time to time, I realize I could have been dead, but I am thankful for grace and mercy intervening. Yes, there are times you may be exhausted from the previous assignment, but please do not make an excuse if the next one comes along prior to you being ready. It is an honor to serve in the kingdom. Therefore, remain hospitable and faithful to your assignments because there is a day of recognition earmarked for you.

38. The Persistent Widow
(Luke 18:1-8)

Comments

This is a widely used or popular parable in the church family. On one hand, we are encouraged to pray, believe, and leave the petition in the hands of the Lord. Alternatively, we are taught to pray in this parable, but it is also appropriate to be insistent and tenacious when it comes to the matter of importance. In other words, God's grace allows you to ask the same thing again and again until you see favorable results.

We should be cognizant of the fact that prayer is a spiritual enabling tool or vehicle which transports our concerns into the presence of God during awkward times. In addition, it does not matter about the socio-economic status of the person making the request because there are resounding benefits for being righteous and humble. In this parable, we are about to observe contrasting lifestyles, such as the righteous and unrighteous or the temporal versus the eternal kingdoms functioning on behalf of a faithful witness. You will also see the legal and spiritual dimensions of righteousness played out under the watchful eyes of the Almighty.

1. What are the circumstances surrounding the origin of this parable?

In the previous chapter, Jesus was on his way to Jerusalem (verse 11). The Pharisees inquired about the Kingdom of God, and Jesus taught the disciples (verse 22) about the *Eschaton* or doctrines of the Last Days. There will be definite signs or benchmarks helping us to realize the Son of Man is about to return. Therefore, the parable serves as a reminder of how we must behave when faced with challenges.

2. Who is the parable addressed to?

I believe the parable is specifically addressed to the disciples. However, there are resounding benefits for the religious leaders and the close multitude.

3. What is the parable drawn from?

The parable is drawn from a common experience.

- The term *Widow* stems from the Old Testament word *Almanah.* It has to do with a woman who has lost her social and economic position because of the death of her husband; a woman needing assistance. The New Testament term *Chera* seems to indicate an elderly woman who was often seen as someone forsaken or in dire need of help.

- The Old Testament term *Sapat* refers to a judge. A judge is an official who delivers a ruling or sentence in legal matters. The New Testament verb *Krino* has to do with separating, selecting, choosing, or determining what is right.

4. Variations in the Gospels.

- This parable is found only in Luke. However, there are similar references expressed in the earlier parable entitled, *The Parable of the Friend in Need* (Luke 11:5-8).

- Jesus unlocks another mystery surrounding the Kingdom of God by telling the disciples praying from the heart remains germane to getting a favorable response. Or you can see faith must be at the core (heart) of praying.

- Jesus drew from a scenario they could relate to, wherein there was an unrighteous judge (that sounds familiar) placed in the seat of authority whom had to be reckoned with.

- In contrast, there was a widow who reverenced God and respected everyone. She was righteous yet was faced with a challenge.

- The widow apparently had an adversary (due to debt), and she had no financial means to settle the matter.

- Therefore, this civil matter prompted her to seek assistance from the courts.

- Initially, the judge ignored her request, just like disinherited people are often treated in the judicial system, every day.

- Nonetheless, the widow was not disheartened by the judge's action because she kept coming, again and again.

- The term *vindicate* is a legal word denoting someone being cleared from accusation, blame or suspicion.

- The widow's persistent tactic eventually caused a favorable reaction from the judge although he was known to have no regards for God or man.

- The judge ruled in her favor (vindicated), and this would require the adversary to leave her alone and alleviating the debt.

- The judge reached this decision simply because he could no longer tolerate the widow continually harassing or vexing him.

- Jesus went on to draw a parallel (verse 7) by reminding the disciples God will reward the righteous if they fervently and persistently petition the Throne of Grace.

- Jesus also makes reference to the value of faith as an essential attribute for those associated with the Son of Man.

5. What applications can we make for our lives?

Within the human arena, there will always be adversaries and vexing moments, especially at the most inopportune times. In many cases, the righteous will have to turn to unrighteous officials surrounding legal matters (criminal and civil cases). It is far better utilizing these avenues than to take matters into your own hands. I find the school of humility is the doorway to blessings consistently throughout the Bible.

6. Can you tell the story in your own words?

This is a dynamic and practical story that draws our attention to the reality of the *Haves & Have Nots* in society. It also paints a picture between the *righteous vs. unrighteous* and *temporal vs. eternal kingdoms*. When it is all said and done, we take note of the benefits or rewards from repeating the same thing over and over, especially when the heart is pure. Prayer is a permanent and effective tool for the Saints of God. The widow put forth the efforts, and it was her sincerity and persistency that moved the heart of God to resolve this situation.

Each of you must face up to your vexing realities and have the wherewithal to petition God on a daily basis until you see the manifestation of His glory in that situation. The African Proverb says, "Bite by bite, the ants will eat the elephant." You must become the catalyst or spiritual transformer between the problem and the victory.

39. The Pharisees and the Tax Collector
(Luke 18:9-14)

Comments

This parable immediately follows the Parable of the Persistent Widow. Jesus emphasized the importance of prayer and believing when faced with adversity. However, in this parable, we observe Jesus continuing the value of prayer but gives another perspective on the same.

Once again, we will see a contrasting view of a Pharisee displaying a form of godliness or self-righteousness versus a Publican admitting in humility his sins before the Lord. Whenever a prayer focuses on itself and accuses someone else of their shortfall, then rest, God is certainly not pleased. Alternatively, God is always inclined to hear and aide those who display a contrite spirit and admit their weakness.

1. What are the circumstances surrounding the origin of this parable?

There appears to be a need for Jesus to teach about whom and what is really important in life. Earlier in the chapter, we observed the parallel between the Judge and Widow, and now we are seeing the contrast between the Pharisee (religious leaders) and the Tax Collector (Sinner or Publican) engaged in prayer. Each of you must be cognizant of your attitude toward one another when we are petitioning God.

2. Who is the parable addressed to?

This is somewhat of a challenge, but I am inclined to say it is addressed to both, the religious leaders and the disciples. I say this, because all parables serve as a spiritual indictment against the religious leaders' failure to adequately represent the Kingdom of God. Furthermore, this parable sends a profound message to the disciples, because Jesus did not want them to become arrogant like the Pharisees, even in the midst of the good deed they were doing.

3. What is the parable drawn from?

This parable is drawn from a common experience versus a scene from nature.

- The New Testament Greek word for Pharisees is *Pharisaios* or the Aramaic word *Pereas* (Daniels 5:28). The term denotes to separate or ascribing to a different life other than the public, based upon religious teaching or to be pious.

- The term *Publican* derives from the New Testament word *Telones,* and refers to a farmer of the tax, toll or custom. They were commonly referred to as sinners or gentiles, and they were hated by the Hebrews because they gathered taxes on behalf of the Roman Government.

4. Variations in the Gospels.

- This parable is found only in Luke.

- Jesus teaches about the inappropriate character of a religious man.

- He went on to show the difference in two men praying in the temple by letting us hear what each one had to say. We applaud both men for praying, but one is appropriate and the other inappropriate.

- The Pharisee began praying with a self-centered spirit (cocky) by throwing off on someone else who was praying, nearby.

- The prejudice was obvious, and this was due in part to the notorious reputation associated with the Tax Collectors.

- Actually, the Pharisee launched a series of accusations at the Tax Collector and other men who did not fit their religious model (verse 11).

- He went on to remind God about his faithfulness, by referring to fasting and tithing. There is nothing worse than performing a good deed with a bad motive.

- In contrast, Jesus tells us the Tax Collector's (verse 13) demeanor and posture was totally different. He stood back, versus being "front and center", and would not elevate his head and eyes. Instead, he displayed a military gesture of honor and respect to the Almighty by giving a smote on the chest, while at the same time asked God to have mercy on him, a sinner.

- The New Testament term *Harmartolos* refers to a sinner or one who misses the mark, an offender, debtor, or fallen condition of men.

- Jesus concludes this parable by letting the people know whose prayer was appropriate and inappropriate.

- The Tax Collector left justified or vindicated instead of the religious leader because there is no tolerance for arrogance in the Kingdom. True power and abundant living is grounded in humility.

5. What applications can we make for our lives?

The message from the kingdom entails praying, fasting, tithing and abstaining from extortion, injustice, adultery and a series of other sinful activities. However, here is a classic example of someone who was expected to know better, but instead the man who was obviously a sinner became aware of his shortfall and repented.

Each of you must guard his or her self against self-righteousness or entitlement even if the person next to you is notorious. None of us own righteousness or controls the spirit of deliverance. Therefore, it is very important that each of us pray sincerely, focus on the Lord, and refrain from throwing off at others.

6. Can you tell the story in your own words?

As a child, I would hear people in church often say, "We know God does not hear a sinner's prayer." However, we definitely know God does not hear a self-righteous prayer. There are always those who position themselves as "holier than thou." It is alright to detest sin but not the sinner. Prayer is a spiritual enabling tool extended to everyone, but it should not be exploited.

When you pray from the heart, such as seen in the Widow and Tax Collector, you then see the favorable results extended to both. The choice is yours: pray self-righteously or pray righteously. Self-righteousness is a sin including the practices of the Tax Collector. There is a sin of commission and the sin of omission. You are condemned by displaying the spirit of the Pharisee more so than what you claim to be. Only one man's prayer was heard and accepted. The choice is yours.

40. The Minas (Pounds)
(Luke 19:11-27)

Comments

We should never lose sight of the fact the term *parable* derives from the Greek word *Parabole*. Generally speaking, the term refers to placing something beside or alongside a message in order to convey a truth. All of the parables in the New Testament shed new light on the Kingdom of God and served as a declaration of divine judgment upon the unworthy.

This parable is similar to the Parable of the Talents (Matthew 25:14-30), but there are differences between the two. Jesus tells a story about a nobleman, a royal person who prepares to leave his household in order to receive special honors at another location. Meanwhile, he distributed pounds or minas to ten servants and expected each of them to invest and was given an increase upon his return. There is a day of reckoning for each of us, so it is best to be responsible and maximize or expand upon what God has assigned your hands to do.

1. What are the circumstances surrounding the origin of this parable?

Earlier in the chapter, we saw Jesus singling out Zaccheus as he passed through Jericho on the way to Jerusalem. There was a large crowd following Jesus and a great expectation that God would restore Israel to "favorite nation" status.

2. Who is the parable addressed to?

The parable seems to be addressed to the multitude and disciples, because they looked up to Jesus for guidance. The parable is also addressed to the religious leaders, who misrepresented the truth.

3. What is the parable drawn from?

- This parable is drawn from a common experience, namely nobleman and pounds.
- The New Testament term *pound* derives from *Litra,* a Latin coin of the metric unit for measuring. The term *Mna* is a Semitic term used for weight and sum of money equivalent to 15 ounces or roughly $20.00.
- The term *Nobleman* derives from a Greek adjective *Basilikos.* It has to do with a royal person, but not necessarily the king; a courier or one in the service of the king.

4. Variations in the Gospels.

- This parable is found only in Luke. However, there is a similar account in Matthew.

- Jesus approached Jerusalem and felt the need to share a story about a certain Nobleman, who reflected His mission in relation to the Kingdom of God.

- A certain Nobleman was making preparation to leave, but prior to departure he called 10 (Law and Responsibility) servants and assigned 10 minas to them. Were each given 10 pounds or were they given one each? And were there actually 10 servants involved in the distribution?

- In addition to giving the minas, each servant was given instruction to trade or seek investment opportunities for gain until the Nobleman returned.

- Meanwhile, the Nobleman departs and enters a territory where he is not warmly received (verse 14).

- Eventually, he returned with *kingly power.* This is a puzzling phrase. Perhaps, it means the Nobleman gained respect and was installed as the territorial leader despite the behavior of the group in the territory. Divine appointments are not based upon opinion polls or popularity contest.

- Upon his return, he summoned each of the servants to give an account for the funds entrusted to them.

- The first came and reported an increase of 10 minas and was told, *Well done.* Furthermore, the servant was promoted to oversee or administer 10 cities.

- The second servant came and reported an increase of 5 minas. His faithfulness resulted in being promoted to oversee 5 cities.

- The third servant came and returned the same amount assigned him prior to the Nobleman's departure. He claimed to be afraid and tried to explain (verse 21).

- The servant's own testimony and laziness condemned him and caused him to receive no reward. In fact, the pound in the hands of the slothful servant was taken from him and given to the servant who had been given oversight of 10 cities.

- This caused a response from those standing near them. They could not see the logic in giving more to the servant who already had been given the most.

- Jesus goes on to give an explanation. The basis of blessings and increased opportunities are not measured by numbers or what you already have on hand. For example, there are those with a small amount who will have that taken from them simply because their characters and attitudes will not allow them to succeed.

- The parable concluded by letting us see the ultimate punishment (death) being carried out against those citizens who did not accept the Lordship or rule of the Nobleman in the region.

5. What applications can we make for our lives?

There will always be socio-economic realities in life to contend with. Each of you will come across people who may or may not like you and choose not to respect your authority. Furthermore, there are those who simply will not like you, and so be it. There is truth in the saying, "You cannot legislate morality" and "You cannot make people like you."

The second part of the parable has to do with the delegation and distribution of money or things. Each of you are given something to work with. There is no tolerance in the Kingdom of God for making excuses.

6. Can you tell the story in your own words?

This parable has resounding benefits for all of us. Jesus was on his way to Jerusalem where he would meet the ultimate challenge, death on the cross. The Nobleman reflects Jesus, the servants represent the church, and the citizens represent the religious leaders who refused to accept him as the Messiah.

There will be rewards and punishments distributed upon the return of the Lord. "The future frightens only those who prefer living in the past." (Dunbar). You were created to expand and maximize in life. You can and must do more, but you cannot afford to allow fate to rob you of your divine destiny. Invest in the Kingdom of God and you will reap phenomenal results.

Summary

Parables should be looked upon as revelatory stories or messages instructing us about the Kingdom of God and the Last Days. They serve as a message of clarity and judgment against a wayward and sinful world, while at the same time provoked hope and inspiration within the faith community.

We must not lose sight of the message at hand, even though from time to time, the characters and situations at hand may be colorful and interesting. Nonetheless, they are placed alongside the message to help you understand spiritual mandates, ethical principles, and practical illustrations that, heretofore, you may have missed or did not fully understand.

Jesus Christ is the *Exemplary One* and was manifested as both Son of God and Son of Man. It is important for us to study and understand what He had to say throughout the Gospel. He is the culmination of theory and practice. The truth is usually disguised and hidden but eventually will come forth. Remain patient and humble so the parables will enable you to enter and live a fulfilling life within the Kingdom of God.

Parables are not myths, human-interest stories, or fables. Instead, they are practical hands on accounts pertaining to wholesome living. We must always learn from the religious leaders by not becoming self-righteous, whereby they refused to embrace the message of Jesus.

Finally, parables are spiritual roadmaps that help us navigate through a temporal and sensuous world, whereby we will come to understand the eternal purpose of the Most High God. Getting acquainted with these stories will bring forth an inner peace and confidence like you have never experienced before.

Getting to Know the Author

Nathaniel J. Stampley is my beloved husband. This romantic relationship began at Saints Academy and College, Lexington, Mississippi in 1969 and resulted in marriage in 1972. We are literally best friends and work together as a team.

For example, he is a visionary and is often coming up with insightful ideas. I, on the other hand, sit back, analyze, and help provide a finishing touch. This publication represents his compassion for truth and scholarship. Even further, you will appreciate a fresh approach regarding spiritual, ethical, and practical realities.

My husband wears many hats, and he wears them very well. He is a pastor, theologian, community organizer, international traveler, humanitarian, and so much more. The list is endless. Far too long, the church community seems to have lost the creativity and fervor our ancestors experienced during the period of American Chattel Slavery. Despite these grueling realities, we also observed the birth of the *Invisible Black Church* and the *Negro Spirituals*.

I can assure this book will stir your spirits and peak your interests when it comes to eternal truth lodged in temporal settings.

He often says, "The Bible deals with people, places, and situations." He reminds us, "The formation of the Bible permeates around the lives of the Hamites and Shemites; both were Black."

This book and other publications are designed to correct many of the fallacies regarding biblical literature, while welcome you to the spiritual and eternal Church. He would love to hear from you via email and encourage you to check out his other publications. I think he is absolutely amazing, and he is delighted that you chose to take this journey with him.

www.ingramcontent.com/pod-product-compliance
Lightning Source LLC
Chambersburg PA
CBHW051827090426
42736CB00011B/1681